WHAT ON EARTH?

The Creatures You Have Never Heard Of!

Stewart McPherson

Don Hanson Charitable Foundation
Linden House, Linden Close, Tunbridge Wells, Kent TN4 8HH, United Kingdom
www.donhansoncharitablefoundation.org

WHAT ON EARTH? The Creatures You Have Never Heard Of!
ISBN 978-1-913631-00-0

All rights reserved. First printed April, 2020
Printed in Slovenia on behalf of Latitude Press Limited

Sincere thanks to Dr. Robert Irving for contributing text and editing this work.

To my darling little sister Sophie,
You are a bit of an unusual creature sometimes, so I dedicate this book to you!
Love you always
Stew

Printed on Forest Stewardship
Council approved paper

FSC
www.fsc.org

MIX
Paper from
responsible sources
FSC® C106600

Special thanks to

The Don Hanson Charitable Foundation

Working to provide knowledge and inspire awareness about nature, science and the conservation of our world.

One copy of this book has been donated to each of 20,000 primary schools across the United Kingdom and her Overseas Territories, and also 4,000 primary schools across Australia.

THE DON HANSON

SCHOOLS
PROGRAM

CHARITABLE FOUNDATION

www.donhansoncharitablefoundation.org

www.hansonbox.org

CONTENTS

CONTENTS

5

LIFE ON EARTH

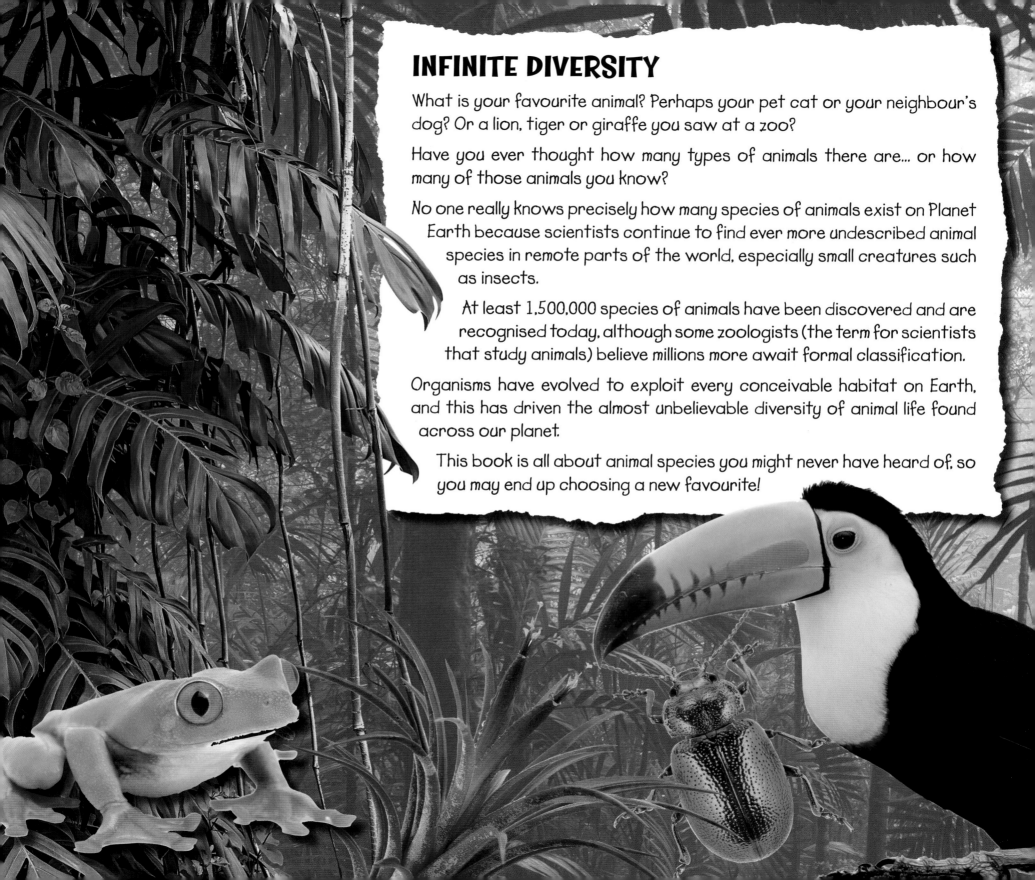

INFINITE DIVERSITY

What is your favourite animal? Perhaps your pet cat or your neighbour's dog? Or a lion, tiger or giraffe you saw at a zoo?

Have you ever thought how many types of animals there are... or how many of those animals you know?

No one really knows precisely how many species of animals exist on Planet Earth because scientists continue to find ever more undescribed animal species in remote parts of the world, especially small creatures such as insects.

At least 1,500,000 species of animals have been discovered and are recognised today, although some zoologists (the term for scientists that study animals) believe millions more await formal classification.

Organisms have evolved to exploit every conceivable habitat on Earth, and this has driven the almost unbelievable diversity of animal life found across our planet.

This book is all about animal species you might never have heard of, so you may end up choosing a new favourite!

OUR ANCIENT WORLD

Planet Earth is at least 4.5 billion years old. That's 4.5 thousand, thousand, thousand years. Just try to imagine this expanse of time!

The earliest traces of life can be seen in rocks that are approximately 4 billion years old.

Over literally billions of generations, life diversified through natural selection into the immense array of organisms that exist today.

But the animals and plants alive now are just the latest versions in lineages that go back through time. Over millions of years, all species evolve, give rise to new species or eventually die out.

If you were to list every species that has ever existed on Earth, scientists estimate that 99 percent would currently be extinct. The dinosaurs are just a few of those hundreds of millions of types of extinct creatures that called Earth home before humans even existed!

DID YOU KNOW?

- A total of about 2 million species of organisms live on Earth today (belonging to all six of the groups described on page 10).

- Millions of other organisms are believed to exist on Earth but have not yet been classified or named (mainly micro-organisms and invertebrates).

- Up to 200 million species are thought to have evolved and become extinct over the last 4 billion years since life emerged! Imagine that past diversity.

GROUPS OF ORGANISMS

For hundreds of years, certain biologists (known as taxonomists) have tried to understand how all organisms on Earth are related to one another. The system that they developed is known as taxonomy and it places similar organisms together into groups based on common characteristics.

All organisms alive today can be divided into six main groups, which are known as domains and kingdoms. These six groups comprise bacteria and archaea (which are microscopic single-celled organisms), protists (which includes all algae), fungi, and all plants and animals (which includes most of the larger organisms we see around us).

Each individual type of organism (known as a "species") can be classified by the hierarchy of groupings to which it belongs.

DOMAINS AND KINGDOMS OF ORGANISMS

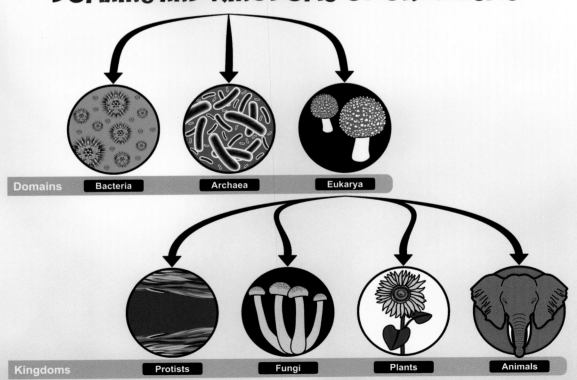

Domains — Bacteria — Archaea — Eukarya

Kingdoms — Protists — Fungi — Plants — Animals

HIERARCHY OF TAXONOMIC CLASSIFICATION

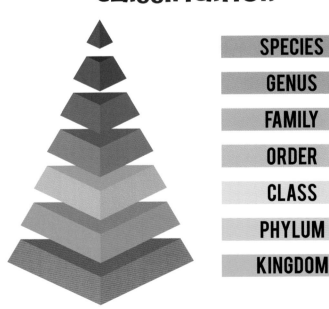

SPECIES
GENUS
FAMILY
ORDER
CLASS
PHYLUM
KINGDOM

BACTERIA

Microscopic, single-celled organisms. Some helpful, some harmful. Amongst first lifeforms.

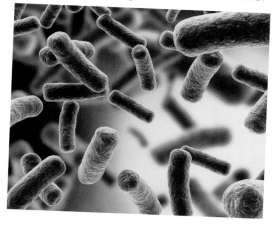

ARCHAEA

Single-celled micro-organisms, like bacteria. Lack a nucleus. Can survive without oxygen.

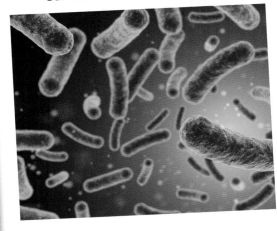

PROTISTS

Diverse collection of organisms. Mostly microscopic. Cells have a nucleus & are highly organised.

FUNGI

Single or multicellular organisms with chitin in their cells. Some live in association with plants.

PLANTS

Multicellular organisms. Most capable of photosynthesis. Possess cell walls with cellulose.

ANIMALS

Multicellular. Consume organic matter, breathe oxygen, able to move, most reproduce sexually.

VERTEBRATES

A vertebrate is an animal that has a spinal cord which in turn is surrounded by either cartilage or bone. The spinal cord is a concentration of nerve fibres carrying messages to and from the brain. The word 'vertebrate' comes from the vertebrae, bones that make up the spine which protects the spinal cord. An internal skeleton and the array of muscles attached to it gives rise to highly developed strength, speed and balance.

There are at least 65,000 species of vertebrates. They are divided into the following main classes: Amphibians, Birds, Fish, Mammals and Reptiles.

Vertebrates are very diverse. Some are adapted to life within the sea, others live under the ground, on the surface or in the air. The largest vertebrate is the biggest animal that's ever lived, the 30 m long blue whale. Vertebrates can also be tiny, such as a species of frog that is the size of a housefly (at just 7.7 mm long).

DID YOU KNOW?

- All birds lay eggs.
- Amphibians, Fish and Reptiles include species that lay eggs and others that give bird to live young.
- All mammals give birth to live young, except just five species (the platypus and four species of echidnas).

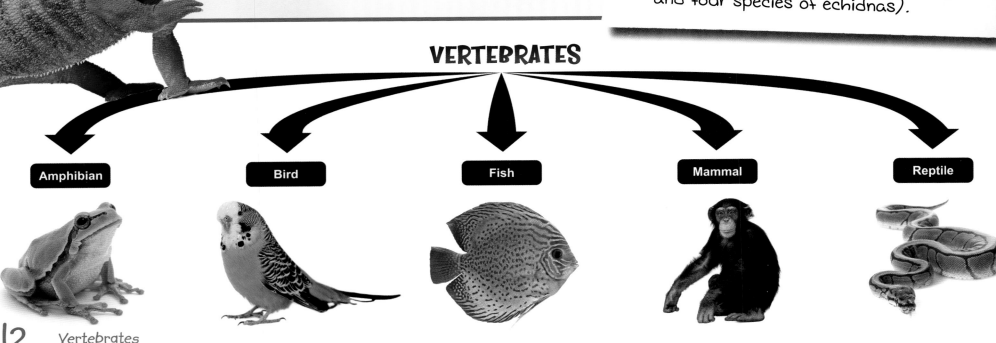

VERTEBRATES

Amphibian   Bird   Fish   Mammal   Reptile

INVERTEBRATES

Invertebrates are animals that lack a backbone. The term (it's no longer recognised as a proper taxon in its own right) includes the arthropods (such as insects, spiders and crustaceans), the molluscs (snails, bivalves, squid and octopus), the echinoderms (starfish and sea urchins) and the worms. There are also many other smaller groups.

Invertebrates make up at least 85% of all animal species on Earth. The simplest invertebrate phylum is represented by the sponges (Porifera), which lack proper organs. They are entirely aquatic and filter feed their planktonic food. Species of the more complex crustaceans, molluscs and echinoderms have evolved external skeletons in the form of carapaces, shells or hardened skins, to protect their internal organs.

Certain insect species (e.g. ants) have evolved a complex way of living socially, where an individual is less important than the colony.

INVERTEBRATES

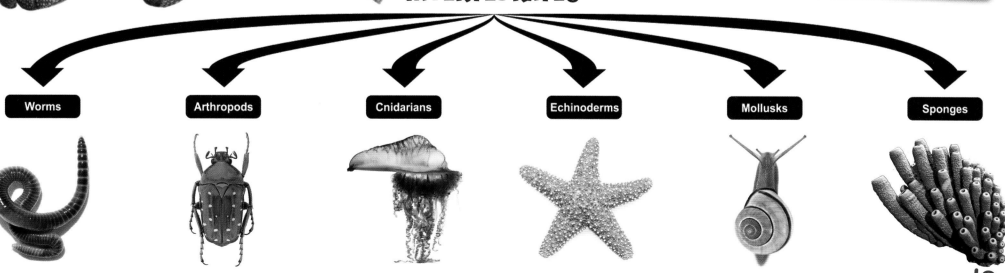

| Worms | Arthropods | Cnidarians | Echinoderms | Mollusks | Sponges |

BIOMES ON LAND

Have you ever wondered why different animals are found in different parts of the world? For example, why are polar bears found only near the icy North Pole and why are tigers found only in the warmer parts of Asia? How come polar bears and tigers aren't found across the whole world?

The answer is complicated. Many other factors play a role in determining where a particular animal lives, but climate is among the most important reasons.

The term "climate" means the long-term average of weather, particularly temperature, humidity, atmospheric pressure, wind, and precipitation (rainfall).

As the climate of different parts of Earth varies very greatly, so do the communities of organisms (known as "biomes") that can be supported. This is because

MAIN TYPES OF CLIMATES

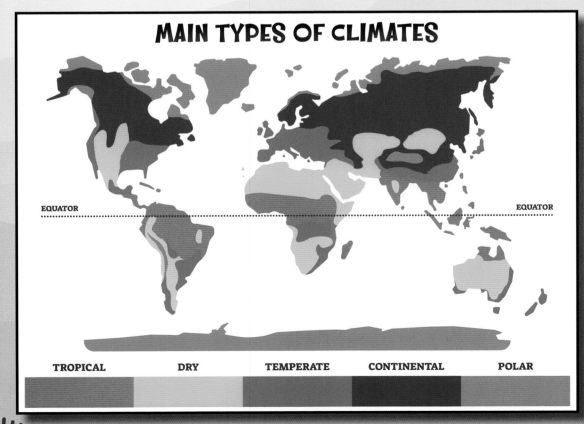

EQUATOR .... EQUATOR

| TROPICAL | DRY | TEMPERATE | CONTINENTAL | POLAR |

MAIN LAND BIOMES

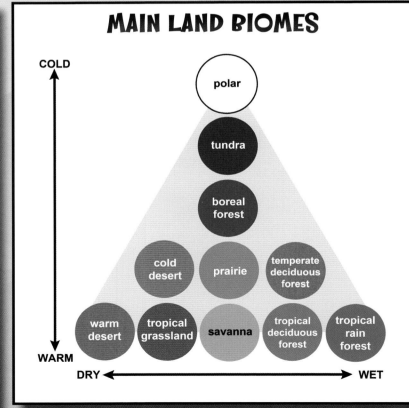

COLD

polar

tundra

boreal forest

cold desert · prairie · temperate deciduous forest

warm desert · tropical grassland · savanna · tropical deciduous forest · tropical rain forest

WARM

DRY ⟷ WET

each biome consists of organisms that are specially adapted to the climatic conditions present in each place on Earth.

Broadly speaking, there are five main climates on land:

1. tropical (warm all year round),
2. polar (cold all year round),
3. temperate (warm summer and cold winter),
4. continental (hot summer and very cold winter),
5. dry (little rainfall),

Within these five main climate types, the variation of temperature and precipitation create 11 principal biomes across the surface of Earth, each with different organisms!

POLAR

Polar habitats are located at the very north (the Arctic) and the very south (the Antarctic) of the globe - regions known as 'the poles'. Here there's just two seasons: summer and winter. It's either 24 hours of daylight or 24 hours of darkness. Temperatures can drop to -50 degrees or more, so it's a pretty hostile place. Very few animals and plants are able to survive in these habitats. Those that can have thick fur or feathers, tend to be coloured white and may hibernate during the coldest months.

TUNDRA

Tundra is the term given to habitats where the ground is nearly always frozen. It's only the top layer that defrosts a little during the summer months. This allows for grasses, mosses and lichens to grow, but there isn't enough room for tree roots in the non-frozen soil. Below this top layer is the permafrost - soil that never thaws at all. Reindeer are one of the few mammals able to survive in these harsh conditions.

BOREAL FOREST

'Boreal' means 'of the far north' and this type of forest grows in the cold regions of northern Russia, Canada and Alaska (USA). It consists of both coniferous and deciduous trees and, like all forest, they are important for absorbing CO_2 from the atmosphere, acting as a 'carbon sink'.

COLD DESERT

Cold deserts have hot summers but extremely cold winters. These deserts are found in high, flat areas, called plateaus, or mountainous areas in the middle of continents (lying between the polar regions and the tropics). Like other types of desert, cold deserts get very little rain or snow. However, they may still be dominated by sand. An example of a cold desert is the Gobi Desert in Mongolia.

PRAIRIE

A prairie is a type of open habitat with mostly grasses, but also flowering plants and occasional shrubs or isolated trees. This type of habitat can be found around the world, but it goes by different names, such as 'steppes' in Asia. The word 'prairie' generally means grasslands in North America.

TEMPERATE DECIDUOUS FOREST

A temperate deciduous forest has four distinct seasons: winter, spring, summer and autumn. Winters are cold and summers are warm. Typically, they get between 75 and 150 cm of rainfall a year, with rainfall likely at any time. These forests tend to be dominated by deciduous trees which shed their leaves during autumn, regrowing new ones the following spring. Animals also have to adapt to the changing seasons.

WARM DESERT

These deserts are lands of extremes: most of them are among the hottest, the driest and the sunniest places on Earth. These are what most people think of as being deserts. They tend to be dominated by sand, which can get blown into huge sand dunes. As very little precipitation occurs, these regions are extremely hostile places for any forms of wildlife. Yet somehow, some species have adapted to survive here.

TROPICAL GRASSLAND

Tropical grasslands are found where there is not enough rainfall to sustain forest growth, but sufficient to prevent the area becoming a desert. The height of the grasses tends to be governed by the amount of rainfall, and the roots of the grasses may extend 1-2 m down from the surface. Tropical grasslands are found particularly in Africa and in northern Australia and New Guinea.

TROPICAL DECIDUOUS FOREST

Tropical deciduous forests occur in regions with heavy rainfall for part of the year, followed by a marked dry season. The forests are dense and lush during the wet summers but become a dry landscape during the dry winters when most trees shed their leaves. Shedding their leaves allows trees to conserve water during dry periods.

SAVANNA

Savanna is a kind of tropical grassland found in Africa. There are usually a few scattered trees present and grass cover varies depending if it's the rainy or dry season. This is where large herds of grazing animals are found (such as zebra and wildebeest), constantly on the lookout for predators.

TROPICAL RAINFOREST

Tropical rainforests provide a hot, moist place to live. They are found either side of the Earth's equator and receive from 60 to 160 inches (150-400 cm) of precipitation throughout the year. Tall, broadleaved trees dominate the canopy layer, with lush vegetation beneath. The world's largest tropical rainforests are in South America (the Amazon), Africa, and Southeast Asia.

AQUATIC BIOMES

This section includes all ecosystems which are dominated by water - collectively referred to as 'aquatic biomes'. They are divided into two main types based on their salinity (the amount of salt dissolved in the water). Thus we have freshwater ecosystems (defined as having a salinity of less than 1%) and marine ecosystems (where the salinity is greater than 1%). Where the two mix (along coasts), we end up with ecosystems such as mudflats, mangroves and saltmarshes. All support diverse assortments of animals and plants.

OCEAN LAYERS

Sunlight Zone

200 m

Twilight Zone

1,000 m

Midnight Zone

4,000 m
Abyssal Zone

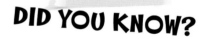

DID YOU KNOW?

- Over 90% of marine species live in the sunlight zone – the abyssal zone is almost lifeless.

- There are estimated to be as many atoms in a teaspoon of water as there are teaspoons of water in the Atlantic Ocean!

Living on land, we take light for granted. From high ground on clear days, we can see views for many miles. In the ocean, even in the clearest water, you would not expect to see more than 40 m horizontally. This is because seawater absorbs light to a much greater degree than air does.

Additionally, much of the sunlight striking the surface of the ocean never penetrates any further; instead it's reflected back into the atmosphere. The amount that's reflected depends upon the time of day, the season and the latitude. At the Equator, the amount of light entering through the surface is fairly stable, but the seasonal variation increases as one moves towards the Poles. The maximum depth to which any light penetrates through the water will depend on the amount of suspended matter in the water column.

SUNLIGHT ZONE

Sunlight is made up of different wavelengths of light, perceived by us as different colours. The longest wavelengths at the red end of the spectrum are absorbed by water first; blue light penetrates the furthest. If you dive down through sea water you would notice the colours gradually diminishing, until everything appeared blue or very dark. And if you're cut during your dive, your blood would appear blue! This mean that organisms that need sunlight to survive (particularly seaweeds and corals), are confined to shallow waters.

TWILIGHT ZONE

By the time you reach the twilight zone, things are pretty dark, with barely enough light to see. It's only possible to detect an organism's true colours if you shine a light on it. Because what light there is always comes from above, many species of fish have evolved a two-tone colour scheme, being lighter on their lower halves and darker above. Thus they merge into their surroundings when viewed by predators from either above or below.

MIDNIGHT AND ABYSSAL ZONES

Welcome to the blackness of eternal night! Senses other than sight become more important down here, especially the ability to detect slight changes in pressure. Not only is it pitch black, the water pressure is immense. Most animals overcome this through consisting mostly of water themselves.

CORAL REEFS

Coral reefs are probably the most vibrant, productive and biodiverse of all marine ecosystems. The reefs primarily are made up of stony coral colonies, each consisting of thousands of minute coral polyps that are capable of producing a calcium carbonate skeleton under a layer of living tissue. Coral reefs are found in shallow, warm water areas around tropical and subtropical coasts.

KELP FORESTS

The term 'kelp' refers to several very large species of brown seaweed. Kelp forests, which provide shelter for many animal species, are only found in cool coastal waters that are rich in nutrients. Many kelp species lose their fronds (leaves) during the winter months, regrowing them again in the spring.

RIVERS

Rivers represent water on the move, flowing in a single direction. Depending on the local rainfall, the type of ground they flow over and the stability of their banks, the water may be clear or very silty. Surviving in this habitat, an animal on the riverbed needs to be able to hold on firmly, and one in the water column must be able to swim against the current. The bonus is that there's usually lots of oxygen dissolved in the water (particularly upstream) and food aplenty.

LAKES

Lakes are large, contained bodies of 'standing' freshwater, usually having an input of water from rivers or streams and some form of outflow (as well as evaporation). A lake is a fairly stable habitat, particularly in its depths. However, in smaller lakes, oxygen may be in short supply (especially during summer months) and the water can become stagnant. In some parts of the world, lakes and ponds provide a vital source of drinking water for many animals.

PONDS

Ponds are also contained bodies of standing freshwater, but they're just smaller and shallower than lakes. With a smaller volume of water, this means they heat up and cool down faster, which the life living within them has to cope with. Ponds may have a relatively short lifespan, as they can become clogged with sediments and plant growth quite quickly. However, they support a wealth of wildlife too.

MANGROVES

Mangrove trees (of which there are about 65 species) are only found in the tropics, typically lining deltas and sheltered estuaries. Mangroves are able to tolerate being inundated by salty seawater every rising tide. They are highly productive, providing a home to thousands of species (including birds, monkeys and insects), both above and below the water line.

MARSHES

Marshes will tend to form where land is continually wet. While many plants can't tolerate having their roots permanently wet, others can and these form a unique wetland habitat which offers food and shelter to a wide range of wildlife, particularly to many bird species.

BRACKISH ESTUARIES

Estuaries form where rivers meet the sea, and thus are a mix of fresh and sea water (referred to as 'brackish'). As a result of the silt brought downstream by the rivers, estuaries tend to be extremely muddy places. For birds and fish in particular, this means abundant food in the form of worms and other invertebrates. Consequently, many estuaries have become nature reserves and excellent places to observe wildlife.

Amphibians are vertebrates that need water, or at least a moist environment, to survive. All can breathe and absorb water through their very thin skin. A few species, such as the lungless salamanders, lack the primitive lungs that other amphibians have and breathe exclusively through their skin!

The term 'amphibian' means 'two lives' and refers to their ability to change form between a tadpole stage and an adult stage, a process known as metamorphosis. They are also all capable of living both in water and on land.

Amphibians are cold-blooded, which means that they are the same temperature as the air or water around them. About 7,400 species of amphibians are known worldwide. Within this group are frogs, toads, salamanders, and newts.

Diplocaulus was a large prehistoric salamander that lived during the Permian Period in North America. It grew up to 1 m in length.

COLOURS AND POISONS

Amphibian skin is quite special. Unusually, it can allow both water and gases (especially oxygen and carbon dioxide) to pass through it. This allows some species to hibernate at the bottom of ponds for weeks at a time without needing to come to the surface to breathe through their mouths.

The skin of frogs varies in colour, from well-camouflaged dappled brown and green, to vivid patterns of bright red or yellow and black to show toxicity and ward off predators. Some frogs can even change colour between night and day, as daylight stimulates the pigment cells causing them to expand or contract. These highly coloured frogs are likely to produce distasteful secretions, which may be strong enough to poison their attackers.

AMPHIBIAN INVADERS

The cane toad is the world's largest toad. It is native to South and Central America. Unusually, its diet includes eating both live and dead prey.

They were introduced into northern Australia in 1935 to eat the beetles which were devastating the sugar cane crop. However, the beetles tended to remain at the top of the sugar cane plants (2 m off the ground), and as toads aren't great climbers, they looked for other prey species. These included native insects, and young native lizards and snakes, whose populations then started to decline.

A single female cane toad can lay up to 20,000 eggs at a time, so the number of cane toads has exploded in Australia and this species is now a non-native pest!

AXOLOTLS

This strange looking creature is a type of salamander which retains its larval features (such as the weird pink frilly gills) into its adult form. They are different from other salamanders in that they live their entire lives under water.

Axolotls originate from a large lake in Mexico, where a legend tells that they are really a god in disguise. They are now bred in captivity and kept as pets, whilst the wild population is critically endangered (as the lake has become polluted). Axolotls have the amazing ability of being able to re-grow their limbs entirely, should one or more be bitten off.

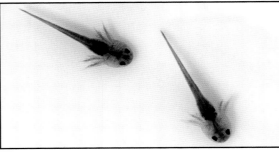

The external gills begin to appear at the tadpole stage. And like many amphibians, being able to grow webbed feet helps a lot with both walking and swimming.

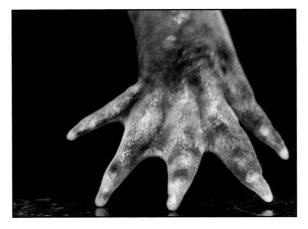

GIANT SALAMANDERS

There are several species of giant salamander which are found in the eastern USA, China and Japan. These beasts are big! In fact, they are the biggest living amphibians in the world.

One species found in south China grows to a whopping 1.8 m in length, feeding at night on fishes, frogs and crustaceans. Individuals in captivity (being fed regularly and properly looked after) have lived for over 50 years.

In China, giant salamanders are becoming quite rare as locals regard them as somewhat of a delicacy to eat. However, they are experimenting with trying to keep them in 'farms', ensuring as many of their tadpole offspring survive as possible.

NEWTS AND SALAMANDERS

Newts and salamanders look very similar but there are subtle differences between the two. However, just to add a bit of possible confusion, newts all belong within the salamander family (so it's still correct to call them salamanders), but not all salamanders are newts!

As adults, newts live a semi-aquatic to aquatic life, while adult salamanders live a mostly terrestrial life, except for when they're breeding and laying eggs. Most newts have webbed feet and a paddle-like tail, which makes it easier to live in the water. And finally, salamanders typically have longer and more rounded tails, and possess well-developed toes for digging in soil.

FLYING FROGS

These should really be called gliding frogs, as they use their webbed feet to act like parachutes to glide from tree to tree. Most 'flying' creatures are capable of upward flight, which these frogs have yet to master.

This gliding ability has evolved several times in different species of frogs, but the most well-known is Wallace's flying frog, described to the world by a specimen caught by the great Alfred Russell Wallace, a contemporary of Charles Darwin. This species, which inhabits dense tropical jungle in Malaysia and Borneo, is an eye-catching bright green on top and bright yellow underneath. It spends most of its time in the tree tops, only descending to the ground to mate and lay eggs.

DID YOU KNOW?

- Flying frogs don't really fly but glide!

- They can glide up to 15 m and do so without making a sound.

- They control their gliding direction by changing the angle of their webbed feet!

GOLIATH FROGS

The goliath frog is the largest living frog on the planet. Individuals can grow up to 32 cm in length and weight up to 3.25 kg. They are found in western African, restricted to the countries of Cameroon and Equatorial Guinea.

The goliath frog is normally found in and near fast-flowing rivers with sandy bottoms. These rivers are typically clear and well oxygenated. The frogs will spend most of the day in the water, venturing on to land at night.

Their egg masses consist of several hundred to a few thousand eggs and, once hatched, it takes about 3 months for the tadpoles to grow into miniature adults.

The tadpoles only feed on one particular plant which is found near waterfalls and rapids, and this may explain their restricted range. The adults feed on spiders, worms and insects, such as locusts and dragonflies. They may also eat baby turtles and young snakes.

Goliath frogs can live up to 15 years in the wild, and 20 years in captivity. They are hunted and eaten by local tribespeople, with some being caught and exported to zoos and to the pet trade. However, they've yet to breed in captivity.

ARROW FROGS

Arrow frogs, also known as poison dart frogs, are native to tropical Central and South America. They are diurnal (meaning they rest at night and are active during the day) and many of them have brightly coloured bodies. The reason for this is as a warning to potential predators, effectively saying, "Don't eat me – I'm poisonous!"

The yellow one shown to the right is the golden poison frog, the most poisonous frog on Earth and capable of killing 10 grown men! But interestingly, the frogs don't make the poison themselves – it comes from their prey of ants, mites and termites.

Native Amerindians have been able to make use of the poisonous secretions to poison the tips of their blow-darts. However, whilst there are over 170 species of arrow frogs, only four are known to have been used for this purpose.

Adult arrow frogs lay their eggs in moist places, including on leaves, in plants, among exposed roots, and elsewhere. Once the eggs hatch, the adult piggybacks the tadpoles, one at a time, to suitable water. This may be either a small pool, or the water gathered in the throat of bromeliad plants. The tadpoles remain there until they metamorphose. For some species, extra unfertilised eggs are laid at regular intervals by the mother, which act as food for the newly-hatched tadpoles.

Sadly, many frog species in tropical countries are becoming infected by a fungal disease, which can be fatal. The fungal spores affect the skin of the frog, preventing the skin from being able to breathe. The world population of amphibians is believed to have declined by 30% as a result of the disease. Scientists are currently trying to find a means of controlling the disease. As a result, a number of these frog species have

BEAUTIFUL BIRDS

There are at least 10,500 species of birds worldwide. They come in many different forms and colours, making them a fascinating group to study. Their main characteristic features are:

- they are covered by feathers (often brightly coloured and patterned);

- the vast majority can fly as they have evolved lightweight skeletons (although about 40 bird species are flightless);

- they have horn-like beaks or bills instead of teeth;

- and they all reproduce by laying eggs. In addition, many species build nests, where the eggs can hatch and the young develop in safety.

Arctic terns perform the longest migration of any animal - an amazing 70,000 km round trip from the Arctic to the Antarctic and back again.

POISONOUS BIRDS

There are a small number of birds that use toxins to defend themselves from predators. No species of bird is known to inject a toxin actively or even to produce venom (like a snake can), but some birds are known to be poisonous to touch or to eat.

Examples include the blue-capped ifrit, the shrikethrush (several species) and the pitohui (at least two species), all of which are native to the tropical forests of New Guinea. All of these birds have poisonous skin and feathers. They do not produce the toxin themselves but get it from a certain beetle they like to eat. The toxin may function both to deter predators and to protect the bird from parasites.

Pictured here is the hooded pitohui (*Pitohui dichrous*).

SEA BIRDS

Many bird species have adapted to life within marine environments. Some nest on precarious cliff ledges to avoid the attentions of hungry land mammals, while others will spend much of their lives simply 'rafting' in large groups on the surface of the sea.

One of the best known seabirds is the penguin. There are 22 species in all, none of which can fly in the air, but they make up for it with their graceful flight under water.

The wandering albatross, found in the Southern Ocean off Antarctica, is the largest and best studied seabird. Its wingspan is over 3 m! It can travel 120,000 km in one year without even touching land - that's 3 times around Antarctica - with it hardly ever having to flap its wings.

BIRDS OF PARADISE

There are 42 species known as birds of paradise and all are confined to the island of New Guinea and to NE Australia. The males are known for their colourful and variously-shaped feathers, which are there especially to impress females. To add to the showing-off, the males perform elaborate dances, which may involve jumping, flapping and hanging upside down!

Many of the tribes of New Guinea traditionally prized these feathers, often incorporating them into their head gear. Pictured here is a Huli wigman.

HUMMINGBIRDS

Hummingbirds are only found on the continents of North and South America. They are called hummingbirds because of the noise their wings make when flapping incredibly fast (as many as 80 wingbeats per second!), which helps to keep the bird stationary (similar to a helicopter hovering). It can then put its long and slender beak into a flower with amazing precision and be able to suck up the nectar at the flower's base. They can flit from one plant to the next at high speed – all you're likely to see is a flash of colour. There are about 360 different species of hummingbird, with many of them occurring in the Andes mountains of South America.

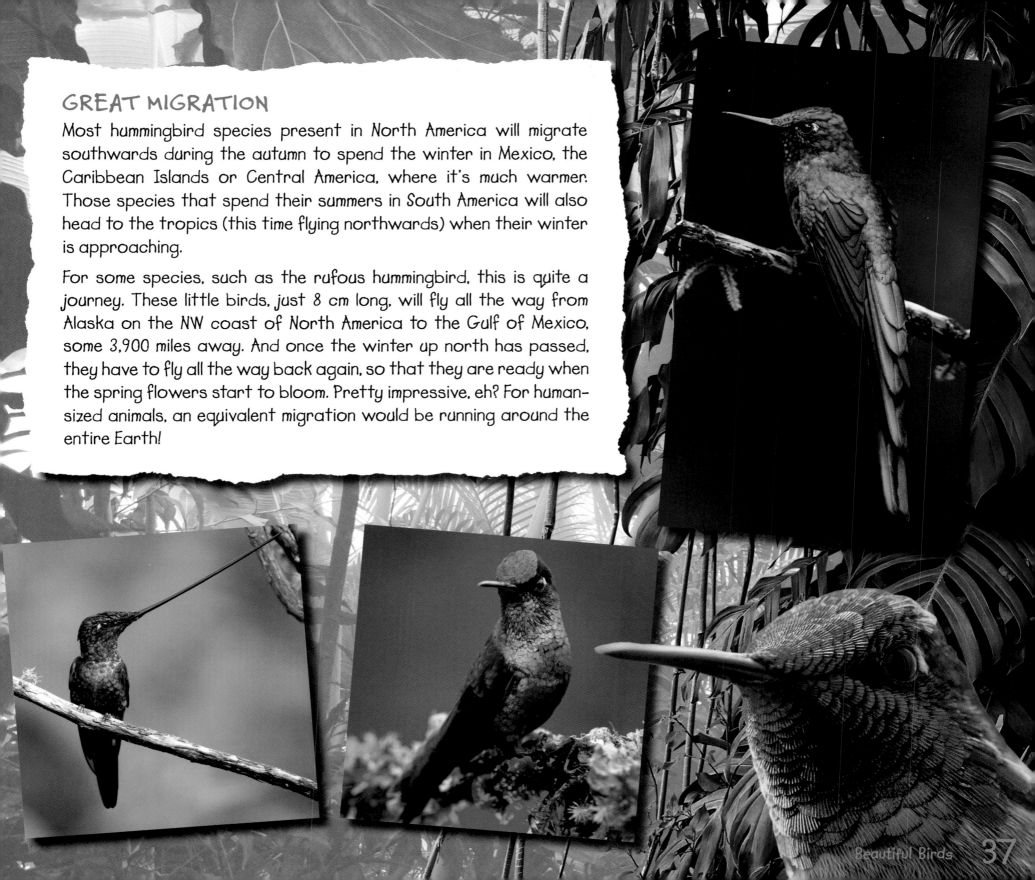

GREAT MIGRATION

Most hummingbird species present in North America will migrate southwards during the autumn to spend the winter in Mexico, the Caribbean Islands or Central America, where it's much warmer. Those species that spend their summers in South America will also head to the tropics (this time flying northwards) when their winter is approaching.

For some species, such as the rufous hummingbird, this is quite a journey. These little birds, just 8 cm long, will fly all the way from Alaska on the NW coast of North America to the Gulf of Mexico, some 3,900 miles away. And once the winter up north has passed, they have to fly all the way back again, so that they are ready when the spring flowers start to bloom. Pretty impressive, eh? For human-sized animals, an equivalent migration would be running around the entire Earth!

RESPLENDENT QUETZALS

This is an amazing bird with a really cool name! It is only found in Central America, from southern Mexico to western Panama, where it inhabits the cloud forest. The most noticeable thing about these birds, apart from their bright colours, are the really long tail feathers which in males can be twice as long as the body of the bird itself.

Resplendent quetzals are primarily fruit-eaters, although they will also eat insects, frogs and the occasional lizard. They particularly like wild avocados which they eat whole and then regurgitate the seed.

Females lay two pale blue eggs in a nest built within a hole of a rotting tree trunk, but sadly only about 30% of the eggs hatch.

PEACOCKS

Although widely known as peacocks, these birds should really be called peafowl, as it's just males (with their impressive tail feathers) that should be called peacocks, with females being called peahens. When courting, the males will attempt to impress females by displaying their impressive tail feathers and shaking them.

TOUCANS

The most impressive thing about toucans are... their bills! Some can be longer than the bird's body, which you'd think would be pretty cumbersome. But the bill is very lightweight, so it doesn't affect their flight too much. Toucans are largely fruit eaters and whilst the bill may help them with this, it's thought to be mostly for showing-off!

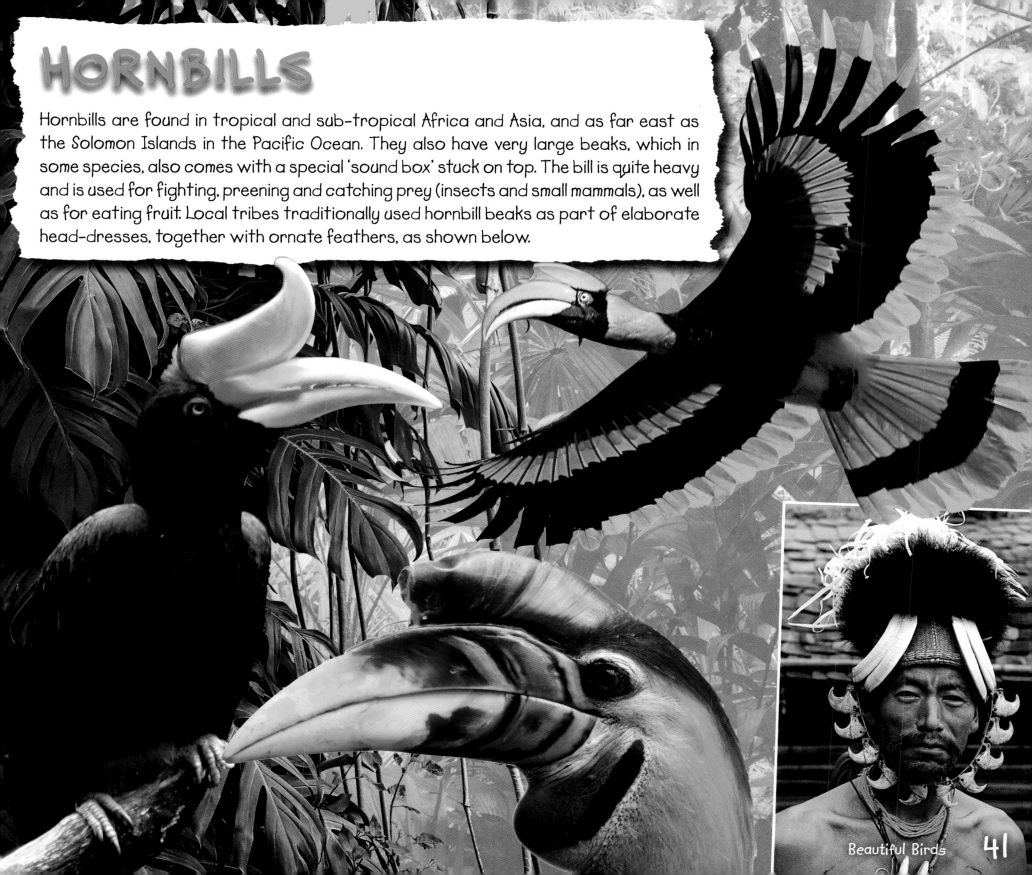

HORNBILLS

Hornbills are found in tropical and sub-tropical Africa and Asia, and as far east as the Solomon Islands in the Pacific Ocean. They also have very large beaks, which in some species, also comes with a special 'sound box' stuck on top. The bill is quite heavy and is used for fighting, preening and catching prey (insects and small mammals), as well as for eating fruit. Local tribes traditionally used hornbill beaks as part of elaborate head-dresses, together with ornate feathers, as shown below.

BEAUTIFUL BIRDS

Birds evolved from small "theropod" dinosaurs which developed increasingly specialised feathers to glide after prey, eventually giving rise to powered flight.

Some of the earliest fossils of recognisable birds with feathers are dated to over 150 million years old, such as *Archaeopteryx* (shown here).

Since their emergence, birds have evolved into a rainbow of diversity! Here are just a few examples.

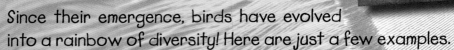

MANDARIN DUCKS are among the most colourful ducks in the world. The males bear feathers of almost every colour, including feathers that are iridescent (reflecting rainbow-like colours). The purpose of this pretty plumage is to impress the girls!

GREATER SAGE-GROUSE males have dramatic pointy feathers but they also have other tricks to impress admiring hens! They perform a "strutting display" (marching with their chests puffed out), and they inflate two yellowish sacs during courtship that look just like balloons!

NICOBAR PIGEONS are known as "liquid metal" birds because both the males and females produce metallic bluish-grey feathers with iridescent gold, copper and green overtones! They are believed to be the closest living relative to the extinct dodo of Mauritius!

Adult male and female GOLDEN PHEASANTS look very different from one another. The males are very colourful and have black and white tail feathers up to 50 cm long, and a bright crimson red and a golden crest! The females are smaller and much less showy, with dull brown and black feathers.

This difference between males and females of the same species is called "sexual dimorphism" and it arises because the males have to compete with other males and "impress" the females in order to mate. Only the biggest, strongest and most colourful males get to reproduce.

The females don't need to compete with one another (since a single male may fertilise multiple females) so the hens do not need the showy feathers!

CASSOWARIES

The cassowary is a flightless bird native to the tropical forests of New Guinea and NE Australia. There are in fact three species, all looking fairly similar apart from their colouration. The one shown here is the southern cassowary, which is the largest of the three and is the third largest bird in the world (behind the ostrich and the emu).

Cassowaries are shy birds, hidden away in dense forest, so not that much is known about them. They have an omnivorous diet, eating mostly fruits, but also capable of taking insects and small mammals. With their large clawed feet and strong bill, they are also one of the most dangerous birds in the world, capable of seriously injuring dogs and people.

It's not known for sure what the horn-like 'casque' on the top of the head is for, although it's been suggested it could help to amplify their call.

SECRETARY BIRDS

This really is an odd-looking bird, though strangely attractive as well. Its English name is thought to come from the Arabic "saqr-et-tair" which means "hawk that flies". It's found in the open grasslands and savannah of sub-Saharan Africa and grows to 1.3 m tall. Its size, eagle-like body and crane-like legs make it easy to identify.

Adult birds have a featherless, orangey-red face and predominantly grey plumage, with black flight feathers and black thighs. But it's the black feathers that stick out at the back of the head which really catch the eye, known as a 'posterior crest'.

Rodents and grasshoppers form the bulk of its diet, but these birds are also known to catch lizards and snakes, killing them by stomping on them.

SHOEBILLS

This strange looking bird is also known as a whale-headed stork, as a result of its massive bill and its long thin legs. It occurs in tropical east Africa, often close to swamps and wetlands. It feeds mostly on fish, but may also take frogs, snakes and even baby crocodiles! It's a very patient predator, often remaining motionless for 10-20 minutes before stabbing at a fish in the murky waters. It is frequently found alongside hippopotamuses, as they tend to force fish close to the surface, where the shoebill can see them.

BONE-EATERS

Also known as bearded vultures or lammergeiers, these birds of prey are the only vertebrates whose diet consists almost entirely of bone. They live and breed on high mountain areas of southern Europe, the Caucasus Mountains, Africa, the Indian sub-continent and Tibet.

These birds have learned to crack bones too large to be swallowed by carrying them in flight to a height of 50–150 m above the ground and then dropping them onto rocks below, which smashes them into smaller pieces and exposes the nutritious marrow. Birds live to an average age of 21 years old.

KIWIS

The kiwi is a flightless bird native to New Zealand. It's about the size of a domestic chicken and belongs to the same group of birds as the ostrich and the emu. There are actually five species.

They use their sense of smell more than their sight to catch their prey, which consists mostly of worms and other small invertebrates. Unusually, their nostrils are located right at the end of the long beak. Their nocturnal behaviour may help them to avoid predation by introduced mammals.

GIANT PETRELS

There are two species of giant petrels, both of which are confined to the southern hemisphere, with breeding colonies on various remote islands. They are extremely aggressive predators and scavengers which has led to their other names of 'stinkers' and 'gluttons'.

As with other petrels, their nostrils are on the tops of their beaks. As a defensive mechanism, they can spit out a foul-smelling oily secretion from their stomachs when threatened. And yes, in case you were wondering, that is blood on the face of this individual - yuk!

FASCINATING FISH

Fish have a very important place in the evolutionary history of life on Earth. The earliest fossils of fish-like creatures are dated at over 530 million years old. These animals were the very first recognizable vertebrates and they gave rise to all of the 33,900 species of fish that are known across the world today.

Around 390 million years ago, ancient lobe-finned fishes began colonising the land and, over millions of years, eventually evolved into amphibians, reptiles, mammals and birds.

It may seem hard to believe, but genetic analysis confirms that all land-based vertebrate animal groups (including primates) have very distant fish-like ancestors!

The wide diversity of fish that exists today comes in almost every shape, size and colour imaginable!

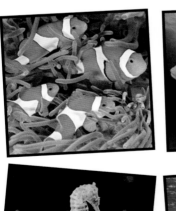

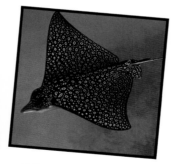

Whale sharks are the world's largest fish, growing to 18m long and weighing up to 19 tonnes. And all this on a diet of minute plankton!

LIVING FOSSIL

The coelacanth (pronounced 'see-la-kanth') is a extremely ancient fish that is thought to have evolved into its current form about 400 million years ago. Only fossils of it were known, and it was thought to have become extinct about 66 million years ago until a live specimen was caught from deep water off South Africa in 1938. A second coelacanth species has since been discovered in 1997 living in the waters of Southeast Asia.

It is their lobed fins which makes them unusual and unlike most present-day fishes. It is thought that those on its underside gradually evolved into legs, whilst it also developed lungs allowing for air breathing, eventually leading to fish ancestors emerging from the sea on to land.

LONGEST LIVING VERTEBRATE

In 2016, this accolade was awarded to a Greenland shark *Somniosus microcephalus*, which was aged as being 272 years old. The previous record was held by a bowhead whale at 211.

It may be there are even older individual Greenland sharks out there in the deep, cold waters of the Arctic Ocean. Intriguingly, scientists managed to age the shark by looking into its eyes and detecting the amount of radiation still present in its tissues from nuclear bomb tests in the 1950s. The shark only grows a few centimetres each year and females don't give birth until after they reach 100 years old!

BARRELEYE FISH

Now this is one really weird fish... There are actually several species of barreleyes living in the deeps of the Atlantic, Pacific and Indian Oceans. It is their eyes which are their most remarkable feature.

The eyes are contained within a dome on the top of the head that is entirely transparent. They are packed full of light-sensitive rod cells but have no cone cells - the ones that can detect colour. The fish can detect the jerking movements of small crustaceans caught by the tentacles of deep-sea siphonophores, yet its sensitive eyes avoid being stung, as they are protected by its transparent skull.

Very few photographs have ever been taken of living barreleye fish. These shots were taken by a deep water submersible operated by the Monterey Bay Aquarium Research Institute.

GOBLIN SHARKS

The Goblin shark, named after a Japanese mythical creature with a long nose, is a deep-sea shark which can grow to 4 m long. Its flabby pink skin and small fins have led scientists to think it swims sluggishly. It is believed to be a particularly ancient type of shark, with a lineage dating back some 125 million years. It is found all around the world and feeds on bony fishes, squid and crustaceans.

EXTENDABLE JAWS

These are what make the goblin shark a fearsome predator. Normally kept hidden below the long snout, its jaws, with their needle-like teeth, are capable of rapidly extending forwards and snapping up prey, before being withdrawn again into the head.

MUDSKIPPERS

There are several species of mudskipper, found on the coasts of Indo-Pacific countries and on the Atlantic coast of Africa. Their eyes are positioned on the top of the head and their pectoral fins are positioned well forward on the body, allowing them to be used like legs. The other remarkable thing about them is their ability to survive out of water. In fact they can spend as much as 3/4 of their lives on land. They can do this by absorbing oxygen through a layer of water trapped in their gills. Their display dances are pretty cool too!

FLYING FISH

There are as many as 64 species of flying fish, most of which occur in tropical or subtropical waters. They use their very large pectoral fins to glide long distances over the sea surface, in order to avoid the attentions of predatory fishes.

Many ray species have also developed this ability, but a little less gracefully. It's not known why rays jump out of the water - it may be a form of display or trying to get rid of pesky parasites.

GLASS CATFISH

Also known as the ghost or phantom catfish, this is a freshwater fish with a transparent body that grows to about 12 cm long. And whilst most catfish species stay close to the bottom, these spend most of their time in midwater. The see-through body provides for great camouflage, and the long barbels on the head may act as electro-magnetic sensors.

SEE-THROUGH CREATURES

Having a see-through body is a great way to hide when you're in open water. It not only protects you from predators, but it also allows you to creep up unseen on your prey! It's a trait that various aquatic species have evolved in different habitats.

SEA DRAGONS

The leafy sea dragon is native to south and west Australia. Its name derives from the seaweed-like extensions which are present all over its body, providing it with perfect camouflage on shallow rocky reefs.

Sea dragons grow to about 22 cm in length. They feed on small crustaceans and planktonic organisms which they suck up through their long snouts.

Sea dragons are closely related to seahorses, and like them, it's the males that look after the 250-odd eggs passed on to him by the female. The eggs hatch from a special brood pouch after about nine weeks.

LAMPREYS

Lampreys are an ancient form of jawless, scaleless fish. There are 38 species worldwide, the largest growing to 80 cm long. They have a single nostril and 7 gill pores. Some migrate from seawater to freshwater, while others spend all of their lives in freshwater. Some species are carnivorous, clinging on to larger fish while eating their flesh, while others don't eat at all once adults.

EXTENDABLE MOUTHS

As a jawless fish, lampreys have evolved a circular mouth (an oral disc) which they can extend forwards to cling on to their prey. The teeth are used for strong attachment. The reinforced tongue then scrapes away at the flesh to get to the body fluids!

HAGFISH

Hagfish are eel-like, jawless fish which are in the same group as the lampreys. They eat dead carcasses on the seabed. They also produce huge quantities of slime from special pores on their skin. They use the slime to escape from any predator that may be stupid enough to try to eat them. If caught, they wriggle so much they literally tie themselves in knots, but the slime makes the knots very easy to undo.

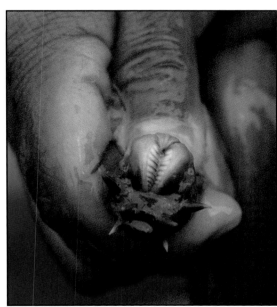

SAWFISH

Sawfish are rays with a very distinct, long and flattened rostrum, lined with sharp teeth that resembles a saw. They grow up to 7 m long.

The saw is used to find prey hidden on or in the seabed, by detecting changes in the electro-magnetic field produced by the target organism.

If prey, such as a fish, is located in the open water, the sawfish makes rapid swipes and slashes with its rostrum to incapacitate or kill its victim!

DID YOU KNOW?

- Five species of sawfish are known worldwide.

- They live in coastal waters shallower than 10 m deep.

- Sawfish numbers are endangered due to overfishing.

SUNFISH

Almost everything is peculiar about this fish. It's flattened from side to side, almost round in outline (apart from two huge, straight fins) and it doesn't have a typical fish tail. Its teeth are fused into a beak-like structure and, unlike most other fishes, it lacks a swim-bladder.

As an adult, the sunfish is taller than it is long, having an average height of 2.5 m (fin-tip to fin-tip) and an average length of 1.8 m, but some individuals are much bigger than this. When fully grown, it is the heaviest bony fish in the world, with some individuals reaching more than 2500 kg in weight. Also, females produce more eggs at one time than any other vertebrate species - up to 300 million at a time!

The sunfish is found in temperate and tropical regions of the three main oceans. They feed mostly on small fish, squid and crustaceans. They, in turn, are attacked and eaten by sea lions, killer whales and sharks.

Whilst we all know that fish swim, some species have chosen to forego this ability in favour of a slower, more stealthy way of moving around.

Frogfishes are strange-looking fish which have highly adapted body forms and matching behaviour too. They generally don't move very much, preferring to lie on the seabed and wait for their prey to come to them. However, when they do need to move, some species are able to walk over the seabed using their specially modified pectoral fins. This adaptation may well have evolved to allow them to move very slowly without being detected by their prey. They are masters of camouflage as well - some species are so well hidden that they have yet to be discovered!

Many frogfish species, with their lie-in-wait lifestyle, use a lure (known as an 'esca') to entice their prey closer. The esca is sometimes held at the end of a thin rod-like appendage resembling a fishing rod. An unsuspecting passer-by will see the lure, be tempted closer by it, and then the would-be predator becomes the prey. In fact, frogfish have the fastest strike speed of any animal on Earth.

Another fish to have mastered the ability to 'walk' is the epaulette shark. This small spotted shark, which grows to about a metre in length, is found along the coasts of eastern Indonesia, New Guinea and tropical Australia. It hunts at night in the intertidal, where it is able to survive being out of the water for up to 3 hours at a time. It uses its pectoral and pelvic fins and wriggling body movements to 'waddle' over rocks, from one rockpool to another in search of its prey of crabs and small fishes.

INCREDIBLE INVERTEBRATES

As introduced on page 13, invertebrates include all animals without a backbone. They make up the overwhelming majority of animal species alive on Earth today. Some estimates suggest that over 85% of all animals are invertebrates!

At least 1,250,000 species of invertebrates are known across the world, and many biologists believe millions of small invertebrates await to be formally named.

Invertebrates come in all shapes, sizes and colours, from featherwing beetles that are less than 1 mm long, to colossal squids that exceed 10 m in length and weigh up to 700 kg!

Amber is sap that from oozed from ancient trees to become solidified then fossilised.

Pieces of amber can be hundreds of millions of years old and often contain invertebrates preserved in perfect detail. Seeing such fossils is akin to peering through a time portal to see long-extinct species!

SMALL BUT DEADLY!

Most invertebrates are harmless to humans, but some have evolved extremely powerful venoms that can kill people!

Spiders and scorpions often come to mind for their venom, but believe it or not, one of the most venomous invertebrates of all is a little cephalopod called the blue-ringed octopus.

Strictly speaking, there are actually at least four species of blue-ringed octopuses and they all live in the tide pools and reefs of the Indian and Pacific Oceans. They are not aggressive and are only dangerous to humans if picked up or provoked.

When angry, bright blue rings appear all over their body and arms as warning signs before they "bite" to release powerful neurotoxin that can lead to death within minutes!

MASTERS OF DISGUISE

Many invertebrates have evolved incredible forms of camouflage! Among the very best are the leaf insects, of the genus *Phyllium*.

Leaf insects live in the jungles of Asia and Australasia and mimic leaves perfectly. They have evolved flat bodies shaped exactly like leaves, and even have veins just like a leaf! In some species, the edges of the insects' bodies have "chew-marks" to look like a leaf that has been nibbled! The level of detail of the camouflage is just unbelievable.

In the 16th century, Antonio Pigafetta became one of the first Western explorers to see a leaf insect! He believed the insects were real leaves that, when dropped from a tree's branches, could walk away on the ground!

SHEDDING SKIN

As you may remember from page 13, all arthropods, have "exoskeletons" of one form or another. These exoskeletons are hard "outer skins" that support the arthropod's body, just like bones support the bodies of vertebrates.

Since the exoskeletons of arthropods are generally hard and cannot stretch, each animal must shed its skin in order to grow - a bit like taking off a suit of armour.

When the armour comes off, the animal expands in size and the new exoskeleton then hardens and forms. This process is known as "shedding" or "moulting".

Amazingly, many arthropods can lose one or more limbs when young, but regrow them the next time they shed their skin! Imagine being able to regrow your legs or arms!

ULTRAVIOLET VISION

Many invertebrates have evolved very different forms of eyesight to ours, so they see the world very differently to humans.

Our eyes cannot see ultraviolet light or infrared light, but many invertebrates, especially insects, can!

For these animals, the world around them must look very different to that which we see. Flowers which look a single colour to our eyes, often have intricate patterns to the eyes of insects.

Imagine being able to see not just the primary colours of light (red, green and blue) but two more as well! Imagine how the world might appear even more colourful!

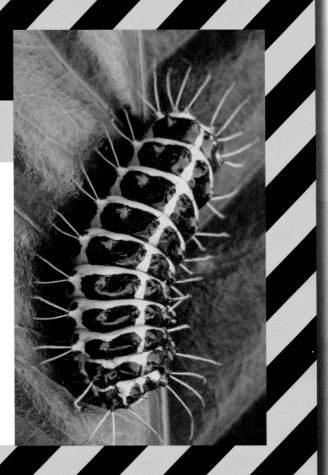

⚠ WARNING SIGNS

Many invertebrates have defensive stings, but in most cases, they usually avoid using their venom or poison unnecessarily because these substances are very expensive (in calories) to make!

Animals with defensive weapons often have bright colours which act as a warning to enemies. Combinations of yellow and black are particularly effective as these colours contrast vividly. Do you go near wasps and bees when you see their colours?

MIMICRY

Some invertebrates use colour not for camouflage or for warning displays, but to mimic species with dangerous defences. This trickery allows the mimic-animal to be feared and left alone by enemies without it having the need to produce defensive weapons! Many caterpillars mimic snakes, for instance, even matching their eye spots!

GLOW-WORMS

Glow-worms are the larvae (and sometimes adult larviform females) of several groups of insects that produce light through chemical bioluminescence.

Many glow-worms use their "glow" to capture prey. Among the most notorious are several species of fungus gnats that produce blue-green light as larvae!

The fungus gnat larvae live on the ceilings of caves and produce many sticky threads that hang downwards. The glowing larvae wait amongst the threads. Small flying insects that enter the caves are attracted to the light and become stuck in the threads to become the glow-worm's meal!

Some of the world's most impressive glow-worm caves are found in New Zealand and can resemble thousands of bright stars!

FIREFLIES

Fireflies are small beetles that belong to the order Lampyridae. More than 2,000 species have been described to date, and they are found in many countries, including the UK.

Fireflies get their name from their ability to produce yellowish-green light from their abdomen. The light is produced mainly by males to attract females.

Different species produce different light displays, usually during the twilight hours after sunset. Many species of fireflies flash their glow by exposing then covering their glow organs.

In Malaysia, several firefly species create synchronised displays, in which, hundreds of individual fireflies will congregate on the same tree, then all flash together to make one big display! Such display trees can flash like a Christmas Tree!

OCEAN BIOLUMINESCENCE

Thousands of organisms create bioluminescent displays in the world's oceans. Many species of jelly fish glow to attract prey like glow-worms. Other animals emit light for camouflage or to confuse attacking enemies.

The most magical of all ocean bioluminescence displays is produced by microscopic organisms called dinoflagellates. These single-celled creatures flash blue when touched or disturbed. The movement of a boat moving through water or waves breaking on the shore can trigger dinoflagellates to bioluminescence, creating trails of sparkling light.

It is thought this spectacular glowing display is intended to startle predators or ward off potential enemies by acting like a "burglar alarm" by making the attacking predator visible and therefore vulnerable to its predators!

The most impressive dinoflagellate displays are found in the Caribbean and especially at Mosquito Bay, on the island of Vieques, where the seashore is known to light up like blue fire!

GLOWING FUNGI

Fungi are neither animals nor plants but are included here amongst organisms that glow because they produce possibly the most eerie and unearthly bioluminescence displays of all.

At least eighty species of fungi are known to glow worldwide, and in all cases, they produce greenish light.

Still to this day, scientists do not know why these fungi glow. Some believe it is a biproduct of the fungi breaking down organic matter. Others hold that the glow attracts animals that could help in dispersing the fungi spores.

BIZARRE BEETLES

Beetles are all around us.

There are more than 400,000 species of beetles known worldwide and countless more that have yet to be named.

Believe it or not, beetles make up at least 25% of all known animal life-forms alive today, and they have existed on Earth for at least 270 million years!

While the majority of beetle species are found in tropical countries, there are more than 4,000 species recorded from the UK alone! Here is a look at some of the most interesting and unusual!

JEWEL BEETLES have iridescent exoskeletons that sparkle with all the colours of the rainbow! Thousands of species are known, and some are even used to make jewellery!

DELICIOUS BEETLE LARVAE

Beetle larvae are considered delicacies in many cultures! Usually, it is the squishy, white larvae that are eaten... would you like one for lunch?

GIRAFFE-NECKED WEEVILS come from Madagascar. The males of this beetle have massively elongated necks which are used for fighting. The male with the longest neck wins!

RHINO AND STAG BEETLES are named for the massive mandibles and horns found on the males of most species which are used for grappling and battling over females.

The Hercules beetle (*Dynastes hercules*, pictured above) is one of the largest beetles alive and can exceed 29 cm in length! It can lift over 100 times its own body weight!

TRILOBITE BEETLES are a very unusual group of beetles in which the females retain a larval form as adults, whereas the mature males resemble regular adult beetles.

Very few animals show such dimorphism in which the adult males and females look completely different!

There are many species of trilobite beetles, and most have spike-like projections along their thorax and abdomen, superficially resembling ancient trilobite fossils!

COLOURFUL SEA SLUGS

Sea slugs (technically known as nudibranchs) are a diverse group of over 3,000 species distributed in seas worldwide. At least 50 species are known from the waters around the British Isles.

As gastropod molluscs, sea slugs are relatives of snails, but they lack shells as adults. Their bodies are lined with feathery gills which are often arranged in rows or plumes.

Sea slugs are famous for being some of the most colourful and flamboyant animals in the sea.

Each species exhibits different colouration, but combinations of flashy pink, intense purple and bright yellow are common.

The first scientists who studied sea slugs thought that the colours had evolved so that each slug could recognise its own species. But it has recently been shown that this is not the case.

Strangely, sea slugs often roam totally exposed to predators. You might think that the bright colours could attract enemies and attacks!

So why are sea slugs so colourful?

Across the animal kingdom, bright colouration generally signifies a message of warning: *I am dangerous!*

This is most apparent among snakes and arrow frogs (see the sections of this book relating to those creatures).

But it has been found that many species of sea slugs don't produce poison or venom directly, although they often do eat animals with stings, including jellyfish and sea anemones.

Amazingly, it has been discovered that many sea slugs absorb and store not just poisons from their prey but even the

stinging cells from their victims which they then re-deploy for their own defence. Many species also accumulate chemicals that create a foul taste!

So, with their technicolour, sea slugs can crawl across the world's seabeds displaying their warnings and few animals dare to attack them!

SLUG-RIDER SHRIMPS

Although sea slugs have evolved a clever way to "borrow" the poisons and stings of their prey, several shrimps have learned how to take advantage of them!

The emperor shrimp (*Periclimenes imperator*) hitches a ride on several species of sea slugs... without them even noticing.

If you're going to get a lift under water, you might as well choose the most colourful and beautiful animal of the ocean, right?

The clever little shrimp gets a free ride to new sources of food and catches morsels while the sea slug is feeding. Meanwhile the poor sea slug gets nothing back in return for carrying its passenger!

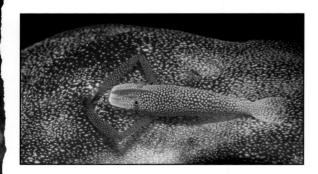

The colouration and patterns of the slug-rider shrimps sometimes perfectly matches the slug on which it lives! The shrimp above matches a Spanish dancer sea slug perfectly!

SOLAR-POWERED SEA SLUGS

Believe it or not, several species of sea slugs derive energy from sunlight!

Elysia chlorotica is the most famous example and lives in shallow saltmarshes and pools along the east coast of North America where it feeds on algae.

Instead of just digesting the algae it consumes, *Elysia chlorotica* sucks out the contents of algae cells and transfers the chloroplasts into its own tissues. Chloroplasts are the parts of the algal cells that turn sunlight into energy through photosynthesis, and so, when exposed to sunlight, they create energy for the sea slug!

This solar-powered sea slug is shaped like a leaf to maximise the exposure of its tissues to sunlight. Some *Elysia chlorotica* slugs have been known to survive using photosynthesis for up to a year at a time! This method of getting energy from "stolen" chloroplasts is known as "kleptoplasty!

NAUTILUSES

Nautiluses are distant relatives of squids and octopuses but belong to a different family, the Nautilidae. As a nautilus grows, it forms a shell that consists of a whorl of chambers. It can adjust the ratio of liquid and gas contained within the chambers, and so control its buoyancy to move vertically up and down just like a submarine! Living nautiluses have been spotted as deep as 700 m below sea level!

Nautiluses scoot backwards by squirting a jet of water form a special siphon, and if threatened, the nautilus can completely withdraw into its hard shell and close the opening with a leathery hood!

The biggest nautiluses can grow to 25 cm in size and may have as many as 90 tentacles (known as "cirri") which they use to scavenge and hunt!

Nautiluses are similar to fossil ammonites but evolved separately, around 200 million years ago. Ammonites evolved earlier than nautiluses but became extinct 60 million years ago. Six species of nautiluses are alive today and have hardly changed for millions of years so may be considered "living fossils".

HORSESHOE CRABS

Horseshoe crabs have hard-domed shells, on the top of which, are two large eyes and five smaller ones. They have a large, grinding mouth in the middle of the underside of their shell, as well as six pairs of legs (two small legs for passing food to the mouth and 10 larger limbs for scurrying and walking). Believe it or not, horseshoe crabs are actually more closely related to spiders than to crabs or lobsters!

LIVING FOSSILS!

The earliest fossils of horseshoe crabs are over 450 million years old – that is 250 million years *older* than the first dinosaurs! And horseshoe crabs are still alive today! What's more, they are virtually identical to those ancient fossils!

Try to comprehend the millions of years that horseshoe crabs have roamed our planet's oceans!

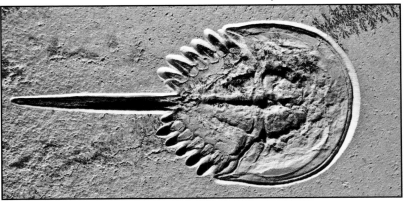

For small insects, tailless whip scorpions are the stuff of nightmares!

These fearsome mini-beasts are found in dark caves and on the underside of large rocks. When hunting, they usually hang facing downwards, unfurl their massive, spikey pedipalps, which act like claws, and wait. As a victim approaches, they use their very long and thin front legs to feel for movements and vibrations, sensing exactly where the prey is, even in complete darkness.

When a victim comes within range, the tailless whip scorpion seizes its prey with its lightning-fast pedipalps, impaling and immobilising it on ferocious spines and bringing it close to its powerful munching mouthparts where it rips the prey to pieces, often while it is still alive!

Can you imagine a scarier predator? Just imagine you are the size of an insect. Think of those fearsome claws snatching at you in the dark!

Despite their terrifying appearance, tailless whip scorpions are virtually harmless to humans. They can't bite or sting but can nip a finger with their pedipalps and jaws. Despite this, in many parts of the world they are kept as pets!

Tailless whip scorpions belong to an ancient group of arthropods that evolved more than 350 million years ago! There are at least 150 species of tailless whip scorpions alive today and the very biggest have leg spans over 27 cm!

Since the delicate limbs of tailless whip scorpions often extend several times the length of their bodies, most species do not have the power to overwhelm animals larger than themselves. As a result, many species lie in wait to gobble up small cave crickets and cockroaches!

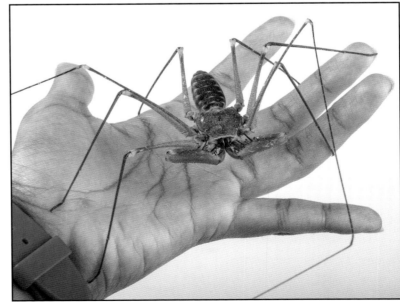

GLOWING SCORPIONS

Over 1,750 species of scorpions are known worldwide, with the largest species growing up to 25 cm long!

All scorpions have venomous stingers on their tails, but contrary to public belief, most scorpions are not dangerous (just painful!). There are only about 25 species of scorpions that produce venom that can be deadly!

Scorpions glow blue-green when exposed to ultraviolet light. Zoologists still don't know the reason why they glow. Some believe this glow shows a reflectivity of UV light and therefore a means of protection in sunlight. Others believe it helps scorpions find or recognise each other, or maybe they do it just to confuse prey or predators.

VINEGAROONS

Scorpions have less well-known cousins called vinegaroons.

Unlike scorpions, vinegaroons don't have venomous stings or claws. Instead, they kill by crushing prey between spikes on the segments of their powerful front limbs. But vinegaroons have a secret weapon that scorpions don't have. They can also spray acetic acid, which stings enemies and produces a vinegar-like smell.

GIANT CENTIPEDES

More than 8,000 species of centipedes are known worldwide. Most are just a few centimetres long but at least 200 species can exceed 10 cm in length and are considered "giant centipedes".

The Amazonian giant centipede (*Scolopendra gigantea*) is the largest centipede alive today and can exceed 30 cm in length, but millions of years ago, enormous species 2 m long roamed the Earth!

The name *centipede* means "hundred foot". In reality, centipedes always have an odd number of pairs of legs due to their body structure, so no centipede actually has exactly 100 legs. Different species of centipedes have varying numbers of legs, ranging from 29 to 355!

Despite having to move so many legs, centipedes can run really quickly and have lightning fast responses. Centipedes have poor eyesight (some species don't even have eyes), but they detect their prey by sensing their movement and vibrations.

DID YOU KNOW?

- Centipedes are carnivorous and have venomous bites!

- Millipedes are herbivores and are harmless.

- Centipedes have one pair of legs per body segment, whereas millipedes have two!

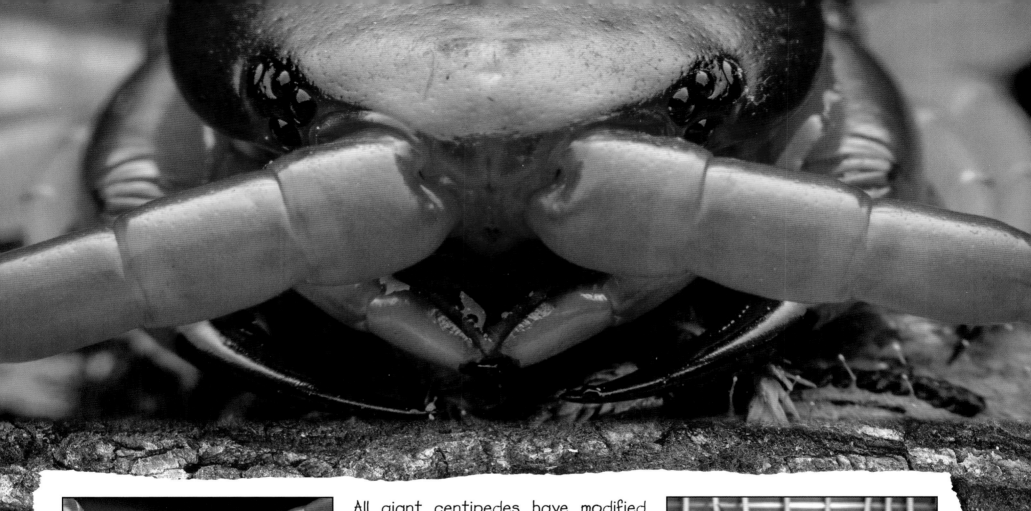

All giant centipedes have modified front legs that form a pair of razor-sharp, pincer-like fangs that inject venom. The venom is usually very painful and may cause severe swelling, chills, fever and overall weakness!

The largest centipedes not only eat invertebrates, but are known to catch lizards, frogs, birds, mice, and even bats!

Believe it or not, in parts of Asia, centipedes are roasted and sold as a snack. Would you like to try one?

CHRISTMAS ISLAND LAND CRABS

Not all crabs live in water!

Across the world, at least 100 species of crabs have adapted to living on land, mainly on tropical and subtropical islands. These land crabs breathe air but must keep their gills moist, and most species need to return to water (usually the ocean) to breed.

Christmas Island, a territory of Australia in the Indian Ocean, is home to the world's largest concentration of land crabs! This island is home to thirteen land crabs species but is famous for harbouring more than 30 million red crabs (*Gecarcoidea natalis*)!

For most of the year, the red crabs live in Christmas Island's forests. However, during the wet season each year, millions of the red crabs migrate to the coast forming a living carpet of red!

When migrating, the red crabs of Christmas Island can march more than one kilometre a day. Nothing stops them: they climb right over rocks and even down sheer cliffs!

The males mate with the females along the way. The females then lay masses of tiny brown eggs which they carry in their abdominal brood pouches.

When they finally reach the ocean, the females cling to rocks and release their eggs into the water. Literally billions and billions of eggs are released each year and armies of countless tiny baby land crabs wash back ashore a few weeks later!

COCONUT CRABS

Coconut crabs (*Birgus latro*) are the largest arthropods alive today that live on land! They can have leg spans over one metre wide and can weigh over four kilograms!

These giant land crabs are actually a species of terrestrial hermit crab! They occur mainly on islands across the Indian and Pacific Oceans, and scavenge fruit, nuts, seeds, carrion and sometimes kill and eat animals smaller than themselves (including rats, birds and other crabs).

Coconut crabs vary enormously in colour between populations and individuals, and may be bright orange, blue, purple or reddish, or a combination of these colours.

DID YOU KNOW?

- Coconut crabs are now endangered across much of their range as people hunt them for their meat.

- Coconut crabs can live for up to 70 years and reach their maximum size after 40–60 years!

Coconut crabs are not aggressive. They are actually quite shy and usually scurry away as soon as they know humans are nearby. Their huge claws cannot reach behind their heads so it is relatively easy to pick up a coconut crab by carefully holding it from behind.

Watch out though! The claws are incredibly powerful and could easily snap your fingers and crush the bones in your arm! Coconut crabs use their mighty claws to break open the shells of coconuts.

Although they are mainly scavengers, on Christmas Island coconut crabs become surrounded by millions of red crabs during the red crab migration events. There, they have learned how to catch and gobble up their smaller red relatives and snack on as many as they can grab!

GIANT WETAS

Wetas are flightless crickets that evolved at least 200 million years ago. They saw the dinosaurs come and go, and once had a wide distribution across Earth, but now most wetas are found only in New Zealand.

Of the 70 or so species of wetas that are alive today, 11 are considered "giant wetas". The largest species is the Little Barrier Island weta (*Deinacrida heteracantha*) which can exceed 70 mm in body length (plus antennae almost as long again). One specimen of this species weighed a record 70 g, placing it amongst the heaviest documented insects in the world and heavier than an adult sparrow!

Most giant wetas are herbivores but defend themselves with their powerful jaws. Many wetas can also kick with their spiny rear legs!

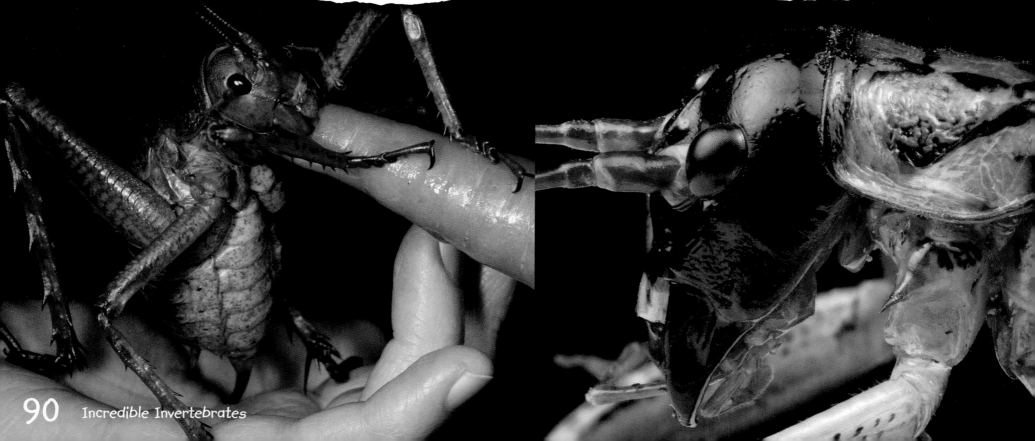

FLATWORMS

Flatworms (known as planarians) are common to many parts of the world. Many species are extremely colourful, especially hammerhead flatworms (*Bipalium*), which use their sensitive head plates to track earthworms, slugs, snails and other prey.

Flatworms have very simple organs, including eyes and a rudimentary brain.

Amazingly, you can cut a flatworm into many pieces and within about two weeks, each piece will regrow into a separate, completely formed flatworm! In fact, some species reproduce almost entirely in the wild by "fragmentation" (naturally getting chopped up and reforming).

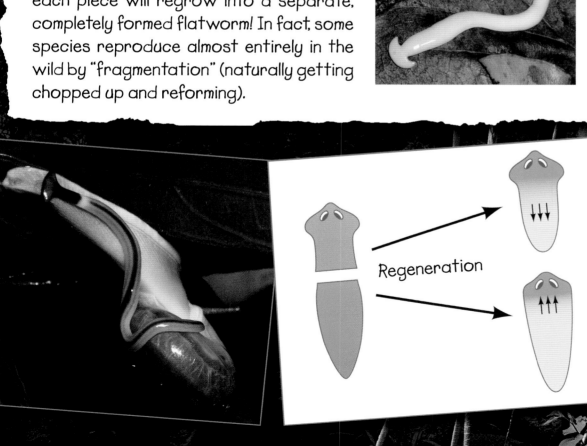

Regeneration

MARVELLOUS MAMMALS

It's mammals that most people think of when 'animals' are mentioned. They are a class of vertebrate animals which are incredibly diverse, and have managed to colonise just about every habitat on earth. The group is characterised by possessing mammary glands which produce milk to feed their young; a body covering of fur or hair (almost absent in some) and having three bones in the middle ear.

There are about 5,500 species of mammals alive today. They come in all shapes and sizes, ranging from the minute Etruscan pygmy shrew (which is just 5 cm and weighs as little as 1.3 g), to the mighty blue whale, (which measures up to 30 m long and weighing 180 tonnes!)

Polar bears are the world's largest carnivores and the only animal known to actively hunt humans (which they only do if they're very hungry!).

OUR CLOSEST RELATIVES

Humans are members of the Great Ape family of primates, which includes the orang-utans, eastern and western gorillas, the common chimpanzee and the bonobo. Collectively, they are often referred to as being our closest relatives and we do indeed share 99% of our DNA with them. However, we are not descended from these mammals – it's more correct to say that we share a common ancestor with them.

Studies have shown that the great apes have complex and intricate social behaviours within their groups, similar to human behaviours developed over the millennia.

AARDVARKS

This *medium-sized*, nocturnal, burrowing *mammal* is native to Africa, roaming over the southern two-thirds of the continent. It has a long, pig-like snout which is used to sniff-out food, primarily ants and termites.

It lives in burrows underground, where it's young are raised. Each toe on its strong legs bears a nail which is flattened and shovel-like, used for demolishing termite mounds and digging out its prey. Like anteaters, it also has a long tongue. Its ears appear disproportionately large, probably helping it to detect approaching predators when its head is down a hole!

Aardvarks grow to 1.3 m in length (up to 2 m if the tail is included) and can weigh as much as 80 kg.

DID YOU KNOW?

- The name 'aardvark' is Afrikaans for 'earth pig'.

- Its nose is made up of more bones than any other mammal.

- They are excellent swimmers.

ANKOLE-WATUSI CATTLE

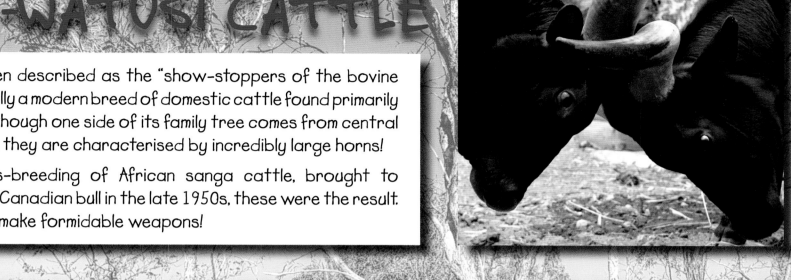

These cattle have been described as the "show-stoppers of the bovine world". They are actually a modern breed of domestic cattle found primarily in the United States, although one side of its family tree comes from central Africa. As you can see, they are characterised by incredibly large horns!

Following some cross-breeding of African sanga cattle, brought to European zoos, with a Canadian bull in the late 1950s, these were the result. Apparently, the horns make formidable weapons!

ANTEATERS

There are four species of anteater, all confined to Central and South America. They are the giant and the silky anteater; and the southern and northern tamandua. All have similar characteristics: elongated snouts equipped with a thin tongue that can be extended to a length greater than the length of the head; tube-shaped mouths with lips but no teeth.; large, curved foreclaws used to tear open ant and termite mounds and for defence; and dense, long fur which protects them from attacks from the insects. All species except the giant anteater have a long, prehensile tail.

An adult and young southern tamandua are pictured to the right. Their log, curved claws are able to grip the trunks of trees, and those of babies are ideal for gripping on to mum's back. The northern tamandua is very similar to the southern one but has a more distinct blackened fur area resembling a sleeveless vest.

The photo below is of a baby giant anteater. This species has an overall grey colouration with a black stripe passing from under its chin to the middle of its back. Giant anteaters grow to over 2 m in length and up to 50 kg in weight. They have poor eyesight, but their sense of smell is reputed to be 40 times more sensitive than that of humans. When walking on the ground, they walk on their front knuckles, in a similar way to gorillas and chimpanzees. Giant anteaters have no teeth, and very little jaw movement - the tongue alone is responsible for all consumption of their insect prey.

ARMADILLOS

Armadillos are closely related to anteaters and sloths. They have a pointy or shovel-shaped snout and small eyes. There are about 20 species, all of which live in the Americas. They range in size from the 15 cm long fairy armadillo, to the 1.5 m long giant armadillo! All armadillos share similar diets: a variety of insects. And they like their sleep too - up to 16 hours in every 24!

The word armadillo means "little armoured one" in Spanish and refers to the bony plates that cover the back, head, legs, and tail of most of these odd-looking creatures.

ARMOUR PLATES

The three-banded armadillo can roll into a perfect ball providing protection on all sides! Wrapped up like this, it can just wait until the danger passes!

ANCIENT ARMADILLOS

Glyptodons were giant cousins of the armadillo that lived in South and Central America during the last ice age. They grew to the size of a medium-sized car! Their diet is thought to have consisted primarily of trees and grasses.

BONGOS

The bongo is a kind of antelope with prominent markings and horns that can grow to almost a metre long. Both males and females grow these horns, which is unusual.

Bongos are present in central Africa, from Sierra Leone in the west to southern Sudan in the east. They live together in herds, ranging from 5-50 individuals, foraging for food together. Their diet is mostly of leaves, but also of flowers, thistles and even twigs.

No other antelope species has such distinct markings, thought to help break up their outline.

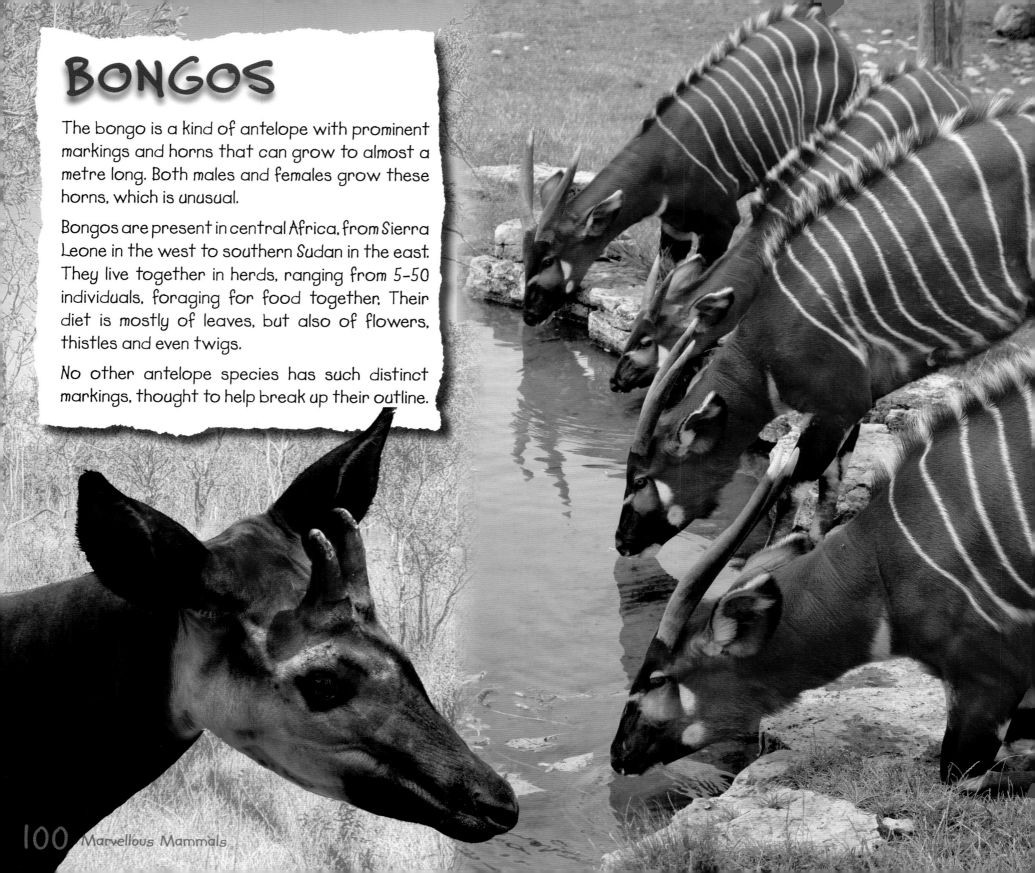

CAPYBARAS

The capybara is the largest living rodent in the world and is native to South America. Its preferred habitat is close to water (it's an excellent swimmer) and it lives in large groups, numbering from 20 to 100 individuals.

Adult capybaras grow to 130 cm in length, up to 60 cm in height, and can weigh as much as 66 kg. You can see that their eyes and nostrils are high up on their heads, allowing these two sense organs to remain out of the water when they're swimming.

Capybaras are herbivores, grazing mainly on grasses and aquatic plants. And get this – they eat their own poo, as apparently the bacteria can help break down the cellulose in the grass they've just eaten.

DID YOU KNOW?

- One of the capybara's closest relatives is the guinea pig.

- As well as being great swimmers, they can hold their breath for up to 5 minutes at a time!

COLUGOS

There is a number of mammals capable of gliding flight, but the colugo is the best of the bunch. Native to the forests of SE Asia, these strange, squirrel-like animals have flaps of skin (a 'patagium') between their legs which allows them to glide for up to 70 m between trees. Even the spaces between their fingers and toes are webbed.

Colugos are shy, nocturnal animals and their diet is entirely vegetarian. They'll eat the leaves, flowers, sap and fruit of favoured trees. They're not that good at climbing back up trees though, having to make progress in a series of hops. They are sometimes referred to as flying lemurs, but they're actually not lemurs at all.

CUSCUSES

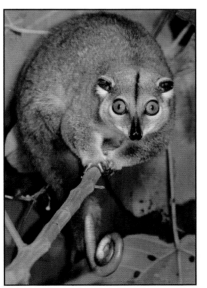

There are four species of Cuscus (not to be confused with the delicious North African dish 'couscous'). These close relatives of possums are found on islands in eastern Indonesia and Papua New Guinea.

They are nocturnal, marsupial mammals that spend their time in tropical, moist lowland forests, feeding on leaves. The long, curled tail acts like a fifth limb, being able to wrap around branches, thereby providing extra stability.

Marvellous Mammals

ECHIDNAS

Four species of echidnas are known from Australia and New Guinea, all of which are covered with sharp spines. Echidnas may resemble European hedgehogs, but they are not closely related.

Echidnas eat ants, termites, worms and insect larvae. They lack teeth and break down their food by grinding it between the bottoms of their mouths and their tongues. While foraging for food, echidnas wander widely and may be exposed to predators. If threatened, echidnas will either curl up into a spikey ball or dig downwards to present the enemy with a carpet of bristling spines.

Along with the platypus, echidnas are the world's only egg-laying mammals (monotremes). The female lays a single soft-shelled, leathery egg that is about 14 mm across. The egg hatches after 10 days and the resulting baby is called a puggle! Puggles grow quickly and lack spines while developing.

FENNEC FOXES

The fennec fox (also known as the desert fox) is native to the Sahara Desert, the Sinai peninsula and the Arabian desert. Its name comes from the Berber-Arabic word "fanak" which means fox. It is the smallest member of the dog family (the Canidae).

Its most noticeable feature are its very large ears. These serve two main purposes. The first is it has extremely good hearing, allowing it to detect its prey of insects and small mammals even when they're hiding underground. The second is that they serve to dissipate heat, with blood vessels close to the skin's surface. The soles of its feet are protected from the hot desert sand by thick fur.

FOSSAS

The fossa is a four-legged carnivore that lives on the island of Madagascar. It is not a cat, nor a dog but evolved separately from a mongoose-like ancestor.

At 80 cm in length, the fossa is the biggest carnivore on Madagascar and it hunts lemurs as well as birds, rodents and reptiles. It can chase its prey and *jump* between trees using strong, retractable claws to grip.

Like all large *mammal* carnivores, the fossa has long, sharp teeth to tackle prey as big (or bigger) than itself.

PLATYPUSES

The platypus has a duck-like bill, a beaver-tail, webbed otter-feet and lays eggs like an echidna! Soon after it was discovered in Australia, a preserved platypus body was sent in 1799 to European naturalists who couldn't believe it to be a real animal, and judged it a fake, made of several animals sewn together!

But the platypus is real. It lives in rivers and streams and uses its extremely sensitive bill to find prey by detecting electric fields they generate when moving. It hunts worms, insect larvae, shrimps and crayfish which it digs out of the riverbed with its snout or catches while swimming.

The platypus has one more unusual trait. It is one of the world's few species of venomous mammals. Male platypuses have spurs on their hind limbs which deliver venom. The venom can't kill humans but is said to cause excruciating pain!

PAINTED DOGS

These are also known as African wild dogs (and go by several other names too) and they are native to sub-Saharan Africa. They are officially an endangered species, as their numbers are declining due to loss of habitat, human persecution and outbreaks of disease.

The painted dog is a highly social animal, living and hunting in packs, and with a strict hierarchy within the pack. They prey mostly on antelope during daylight hours, chasing the target animal until it's too exhausted to run any further. Individuals will regurgitate food for others in the pack to feed on. Their main enemies are lions and hyenas.

SNUB-NOSED MONKEYS

Snub-nosed monkeys are confined to mountainous areas of southern China, Tibet and northern Myanmar. As these areas are often inaccessible to naturalists, not that much is known about these monkeys. That said, it's known they live in large troupes, up to 600 strong. Groups consist of many more males than females. They use their voices a lot to communicate with each other. They feed on tree needles, bamboo buds, fruits and leaves.

JERBOAS

Looking a little bit like miniature kangaroos (and hopping like them too), jerboas are found in hot desert habitats, such as are found in northern Africa, Arabia and Asia.

There are at least 33 species of jerboa, all displaying slight modifications in their features. Some have large ears, some small, but they all have long tails which help with their balance.

Jerboas are crepuscular, meaning that they are most active at twilight. They eat mostly plant material but may also take insects. During the heat of the day, they shelter in burrows. They are solitary creatures.

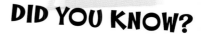

DID YOU KNOW?

- When chased, jerboas can travel at 15 mph.

- They live for about 6 years.

- The tail of a jerboa can be longer than its head and body.

- Jerboa fur is fine and usually the colour of sand.

PANGOLINS

Pangolins may look like reptiles, but they really are mammals! Their large plate-like scales are made of keratin which is the same substance that your nails and hair are made of!

Eight species of pangolins occur across Africa and Asia, but sadly, all eight are severely threatened in the wild due to illegal poaching for their meat and scales which are used in traditional Chinese medicine.

Pangolins are insectivorous and mainly feed on ants and termites in a manner akin to anteaters. They use their powerful forelimbs to break open ant and termite nests and have a long sticky tongue to consume up to 200 g of insects per day!

ARMOUR PLATES

The keratin scales of pangolins form a very effective suit of armour. Each plate is very tough overlapping on all sides with other plates nearby.

If threatened, pangolins can roll into a tight ball and so be protected on all sides by their scaly armour!

Few enemies can penetrate the pangolins' defence. These lions can't seem to work out what they have in their paws.

BLINDMOLE RATS

There are several rodents referred to as mole rats but here we're concentrating on those that are totally blind, which means a group of 8 species. This group are native to the Middle East, the Horn of Africa and SE Europe.

They are blind because their small eyes are completely covered by a layer of skin. As they rarely come out of their burrows, this would seem a sensible rouse to have come up with. What good are eyes in the pitch black of a tunnel? And guess how they dig those tunnels? Not by using their forearms, as you might expect, but by relying entirely on their very large incisor teeth.

DID YOU KNOW?

- Despite being blind, mole rats are still able to keep an accurate circadian rhythm – that is, they know when it's day and when it's night.

- Mole rat burrows can be extremely long – one was measured at over 1 km in length!

PROBOSCIS MONKEYS

Proboscis monkeys are the primate world's most prolific swimmers. They need to be, as they regularly have to cross creeks by leaping from one tree to another, and they don't always make it. Fortunately, they have evolved webbed feet and hands to ensure they can swim rapidly away from hungry crocodiles that lie in wait for them.

The proboscis monkey is endemic to the SE Asian island of Borneo, where they live in amongst mangrove trees. The local name for them means 'Dutchman' on account of their distinctive noses and protruding stomachs resembling early Dutch colonisers.

SAIGA ANTELOPES

The most prominent feature of the saiga antelope is its nose. It is believed this has evolved into its present shape to filter out dust during summer migrations, to act as a heat dissipator, and, during wintertime, to warm up cold air being breathed in.

Saiga grow to about 80 cm tall at the shoulder and weigh up to 65 kg. Their range has contracted greatly, so that they are now only found in parts of Russia and Kazakhstan. It is regarded as being critically endangered.

STAR-NOSED MOLES

Imagine looking in a mirror to see your nose like this! The star-nosed mole has turned its nose into a super-sensory organ for catching worms and insects. And it's reputed to be the fastest eater in the world, gobbling down its prey in a quarter of a second!

Its highly sensitive star organ is constantly on the move, detecting what is edible and what is not within a fraction of a second. And it can even smell under water!

The star-nosed mole lives in wetland and marshy areas of northern North America, and is active during the day and at night.

TARSIERS AND SLOW LORISES

Tarsiers include six or more species of leaping primates, which are intermediary between lemurs and monkeys. They are found on various islands in SE Asia including the Philippines. The body grows to a maximum of 16 cm in length, but the tail can be twice as long as this. Tarsiers are lemur-like in being nocturnal but, unlike lemurs, they have dry noses. They have long ankle bones (tarsals, hence the name tarsier), and a round head that can be rotated 180 degrees. And their stand-out feature? Their glaringly-obvious eyes of course!

Slow lorises (shown here bottom right) are also found in SE Asia. There are thought to be eight species in their group. Their hands and feet are specially adapted to allow them to maintain a tight grip for a long period of time - they stay motionless when threatened. They are one of the few mammals that has a toxic bite, but they use this as a deterrent and not for attacking prey. They are omnivorous, eating insects, fruit and other vegetation. Their numbers are threatened by habitat loss and the 'black market' in wildlife trade.

OKAPIS

The nearest relative of this horse-like mammal is the giraffe, so it has another name of the zebra giraffe. They are only found in one area of western Africa - the forests of northeastern Democratic Republic of Congo.

Okapis are only active during the day. They feed on the leaves, buds and shoots of forest plants, as well as grasses, fruits, ferns and fungi. They also eat a type of clay that fulfils the animal's mineral and salt requirements. Just the males have short horn-like protuberances on their heads.

TAPIRS

Tapirs are medium-sized mammals (about the size of a pig) that resemble a wild boar with a short trunk-like snout. Their closest relatives are, in fact, horses and rhinoceroses. Their lineage is an ancient one, and it's thought they have changed little over tens of millions of years. There are five recognised species of tapir.

Their most distinctive feature is the snout, which is flexible (like an elephant's trunk), being an extension of the nose and upper lip.

Tapirs use their snouts to grab and pull leaves off trees and place them in their mouths. They can also use their trunks as snorkels when swimming in pools and rivers.

Most tapir species live in South America, but there is one (the Malaysian tapir) which inhabits the forests of Myanmar, Thailand, Malaysia and Sumatra. Tapirs graze together in groups, but they don't seem to show much social interaction.

The females have a long pregnancy of 13 months before giving birth to a single calf. These are well camouflaged with their white and brown markings. As they grow older, they lose their stripes. It is thought adults can live for 25-30 years.

If you want to celebrate tapirs, World Tapir Day is on 27th April each year!

TASMANIAN DEVILS

The size of a small dog, the Tasmanian devil is the largest carnivorous marsupial in the world. It earned its common name because of its blood-curdling screams and snarls!

The Tasmanian devil was once native to mainland Australia but is now found in the wild only on the island state of Tasmania. It has a muscular, stocky build, black fur, pungent odour, a keen sense of smell and is ferocious when feeding.

The Tasmanian devil's large head and neck allow it to generate one of the strongest bite forces of all living land mammals. This strong bite allows these devils to eat all parts of their prey, including even the bones! There are stories of Tasmanian devils gobbling up the bodies of murder victims left in the bush!

Tasmanian devils naturally prey on animals up to the size of small kangaroos, but they tend to eat mostly carrion (animals already dead). They are known to take small domestic mammals, including sheep, chickens and geese! They can gobble up 15% of their body weight in a day, although if presented with more, they can eat up to 40% of their body weight.

Sadly, since 1996, wild devils have been suffering from a facial tumour disease which is a form of contagious cancer (meaning it can pass from one animal to another). Scientists are working on producing a vaccine which should protect individuals from catching the disease and have established several "back up" populations to keep the Tasmanian devil safe from extinction.

The Tasmanian devil had a larger relative called the Thylacine (pictured below) or Tasmanian tiger which resembled a large, dog but evolved completely separately from the dog family.

Numbers of the Tasmanian tiger are thought to have been in decline as long as 2,000 years ago, as a result of over-hunting by native Aborigines, and then, more recently, it was shot as a pest by European settlers. The last Tasmanian tiger died in 1936 and the species is now extinct.

AYE AYES

The aye-aye is the world's largest nocturnal lemur, native to Madagascar. It has rodent-like teeth (which grow continuously), and a special thin and long middle finger.

It has an unusual way of finding food. It uses its middle finger to tap on trees to find grubs. It'll then gnaw a small hole in the wood, insert its finger into the hole, and pull the grubs out. It therefore fills the same ecological niche as a woodpecker.

THE ZEBRA WITH SPOTS

As I'm sure you know, every now and then, things don't always happen as expected. This was the case in September 2019 when, just by chance, a tourist saw a young zebra in Kenya's Maasai Mara National Reserve that looked a bit different. For a start it was a beautiful brown colour, and then it had spots instead of stripes!

The baby zebra, which was given the name of Tira, was found to have a genetic condition known as 'pseudomelanism'. This is where the production of melanin, the skin-darkening pigment, went awry, with too much being produced. Consequently, the whites stripes didn't quite happen as expected.

REMARKABLE REPTILES

Reptiles are air-breathing vertebrates covered in special skin made up of scales, bony plates, or a combination of both. At least 10,700 species are known worldwide, including lizards, snakes, crocodiles, turtles, and tortoises.

Unlike amphibians, reptiles do not have an aquatic larval stage. Most lay eggs although a few are capable of 'live births'. Most are unable to control the temperature of their bodies and rely on the sun's heat to warm them up. They are often referred to as being 'cold-blooded' but this is misleading: after an hour or two of sunbathing, an iguana's blood can be as warm as the blood of mammals! They are found on land and in aquatic habitats, and a few extinct species were capable of flight.

Saltwater crocodiles have the most powerful bite force in the world, at 3,700 pounds per square inch! Humans have a bite force of 200 psi!

GIANT REPTILES

Reptiles, particularly those that are supported in their natural habitat by water, can grow to some phenomenal sizes. Top of the lot is the saltwater crocodile which weighs in at a maximum weight of 1075 kg and a max. length of 6 m. Next come the American alligator (1000 kg) and the gharial (at 977 kg).

Sea turtles also display some impressive credentials. The largest leatherback turtle was weighed at 932 kg, and the largest loggerhead at 545 kg.

The honour of being the largest truly terrestrial reptile goes to the Galapagos giant tortoise (with a max. weight of 400 kg), closely followed by the Aldabra giant tortoise (at 360 kg).

The snakes come in next, with the green anaconda (8.8 m long and 227 kg in weight) just out-doing the weight of the reticulated python (10 m long and 158 kg as a max. weight). Finally, there are the monitor lizards, and the largest of these is the Komodo dragon, weighing in at an impressive 166 kg with a max. length of 3.1 m.

SHEDDING SKIN

We humans shed our skin but it's a process we don't notice, as it happens cell by cell. With snakes and lizards it's a bit different. Their skin doesn't grow as the animal underneath grows. So they have to shed it periodically and grow a new skin underneath.

To get rid of the old one, a snake will rub its head against a hard object, split the old skin and then pass through the shed skin, effectively turning it inside-out. For lizards, with four awkwardly-placed limbs sticking out, they have to rub their whole body against a hard object, causing the skin to tear into pieces and eventually fall off.

The skin is shed to allow for growth and also to get rid of any parasites which may have attached to it.

INFRARED AND ULTRAVIOLET VISION

Many snakes have evolved the ability to sense infrared thermal radiation apparent as heat. Snakes with ability have "heat pit" organs close to the end of the snout. It is believed these snakes can visualise thermal images of prey, similar to the image to the left.

Some snakes that hunt during the day have lenses in their eyes that block ultraviolet (UV) light. This allows the snake to see clearly in bright conditions.

Other snakes that hunt at night have the opposite: lenses that let in *more* ultraviolet light, thereby helping them to see in the dark.

heat pits

AMAZING COLOURS

Chameleons are famous for their seemingly magical ability to change their skin colour. Some species really can become virtually any colour of the rainbow within just a few seconds. They have evolved this ability in order to convey emotions (especially when rival males face off against each other), to startle enemies or to enhance their camouflage (see page 41).

Many other reptiles also have the ability to either change their skin colour or to increase or decrease the brightness or contrast of their skin patterns. These less well known colour-changers include geckos, anoles and even a few species of snakes, such as the Papuan python (*Apodora papuana*) which can turn from black to mustard yellow!

INCREDIBLE GECKO GRIP!

Geckos (and related reptiles) have extraordinary feet that enable them to walk up a smooth glass window seemingly defying gravity!

They have this ability because the bottom of their toe pads are covered in millions of tiny hairs (called setae).

The little hairs work together like a suction cup giving the gecko grip even on perfectly smooth surfaces!

ALLIGATOR SNAPPING TURTLES

The alligator snapping turtle is a species of freshwater turtle native to the south-east region of the United States. Its name reflects its immensely powerful jaws and the distinct ridges on its shell that are similar in appearance to the rough, rigid skin of an alligator.

These snapping turtles grow to a considerable size. The largest was measured at well over 100 kg in weight and almost 80 cm in length. Males are usually larger than females.

These are ambush predators. The inside of the turtle's mouth is camouflaged, and it possesses a worm-shaped appendage on the tip of its tongue used to lure fish. The turtle hunts by lying motionless in the water with its mouth wide open. The vermiform tongue imitates the movements of a worm, luring prey to the turtle's mouth. The mouth is then closed with tremendous speed and force, completing the ambush.

These snapping turtles are opportunistic feeders though almost 100% carnivorous. Basically, they'll take anything they can!

DID YOU KNOW?

- The sex-ratio of hatchlings depends on the temperature at which the eggs are incubated.

- In several US states, wild populations are classified as endangered

There is some suggestion that these armour-plated giants may live to 200 years old, but 80-120 years old is the oldest proved age so far. They mature around 12 years old, and will mate in the spring, with the female building a nest and laying 10-50 eggs some two months later. Hatchlings appear in early autumn.

In the USA, alligator snapping turtles are sold in the exotic pet trade by breeders (not from wild populations). Whilst being fairly placid, if they get annoyed, they have been known to bite off fingers with their powerful bite!

ANOLES

Anoles are a group of smallish lizards consisting of about 45 species, although close relatives bring the whole number up to about 150. They are found in both North and South America.

The large number of species reflects their ability to adapt to new habitats and evolve into new forms. Some are spectacularly colourful.

One of the most recognisable species is the green or Carolina anole (*Anola carolinensis*). This is a favourite species to keep as a pet. It has the ability to change colour from green to brown and back again, depending on its mood.

THROAT SIGNALS

Male anoles are highly territorial and will fight with other males to defend their territory. To help impress a rival, they will extend their brightly coloured 'dewlap', a special extension of skin under the chin, and bob their head up and down. If that doesn't work, they'll start fighting.

The fan-throated lizard (*Sitana ponticeriana*) is found in India and has a similar way of communicating with a throat fan as anoles do.

ARMADILLO GIRDLED LIZARDS

This species of lizard is confined to desert areas along the western coasts of South Africa. It grows to about 10 cm in length and lives in groups of up to 50 or so individuals. It hides away in crevices out of the midday sun but hunts its prey (typically termites) during daylight.

This heavily protected lizard exhibits an unusual behaviour when threatened. It will take its tail into its mouth and roll up into a ball. In this way, it is protected from predators by its thick, squarish scales. Its resemblance to an armadillo (p98) when doing this, gives it its common name.

EARLESS MONITOR LIZARDS

The earless monitor lizard is found only on the island of Borneo. It lives close to streams or marshes usually within rainforests. Despite their name, they are able to hear – but they lack ear openings and ear drums. They grow to about 40 cm in length (including the tail) and are nocturnal, spending their days hiding under logs or within burrows. They also spend time in water. Their diet is varied, mostly consisting of worms and small fish.

BASILISK LIZARD

This lizard has developed a special strategy to be able to catch its prey, and it's resulted in its other common name: the Jesus Christ lizard.

It lives its life in the tropical rainforests of Central America, from southern Mexico to Panama, spending much of its time in trees, though never far from water. It can be distinguished from other lizard species by the high, fin-like crest along its back. Males also have similar crests on the head and tail.

DID YOU KNOW?

- Basilisk lizards can stay under water for up to 30 minutes.

- Their speed when running on water is about 7 m/sec (or 15 mph).

- Its tail accounts for 70% of its total length.

Its ability to run on water is the basilisk's secret weapon. When startled, it can escape by speeding to the nearest edge of water – and simply continuing to run. It runs only on its hind legs in an erect position, holding its fore legs to its sides. The tail helps with balance too. The basilisk is adroit on water because its feet are large and equipped with flaps of skin along the toes that allow it to ride on tiny air bubbles. By moving quickly, the lizard can cross a surface of water before it sinks.

Basilisk lizards have many natural predators, particularly large reptiles, birds, and some mammals. To avoid these, it can conceal itself under leaves on the forest floor and can remain motionless for a long time.

LEAF-TAILED GECKOS

Leaf-tailed geckos are nocturnal, forest-dwelling lizards only found in Madagascar and its neighbouring oceanic islands. They all belong to the genus *Uroplatus* and range in size from less than 10 cm to more than 30 cm. Many gecko species cannot blink and need to use their tongues to keep their eyes clean and moist. They have a fixed lens within each iris that enlarges in darkness to let in more light. Leaf-tailed geckos also have a range of vocalisations, ranging from chirping or clicking sounds to hissing noises.

Unlike most lizards, geckos are usually nocturnal.

SPOT THE GECKOS

Leaf-tailed gecko have evolved amazing camouflage to help them blend in with their surroundings. Not only does this involve colour changes but also the outline shape of the body. The leaf-tailed gecko is one of the best at this.

During the day, branches, tree trunks and leaf litter provide areas of camouflage where these geckos can rest out of sight.

CHAMELEONS

Chameleons are a highly specialised group of lizards of which there are about 200 species. They appear to possess a number of superpowers: they can change colour; their eyes are independently mobile; they have an extensible tongue; they have a mesmerizing swaying gait; and some have crests or horns on their brow and snout.

Chameleons are adapted for climbing and visual hunting. They live in warm habitats, from tropical rainforests to deserts.

CHAMELEON SUPER POWERS

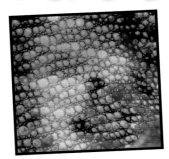

One of the chameleon's amazing superpowers is its ability to aim, release and retract that tongue. Not only is it incredibly accurate, but it's ejected incredibly fast, reaching its target in 0.07 seconds! The sticky end makes sure the target reaches a sticky end too!

INCREDIBLE COLOURS

Chameleon skin has a top layer which contains pigments, under which is a layer of special crystals. Colour changes occur when the space between the crystals is altered. This in turn changes the wavelength of light reflected, and we see different colours.

WORLD'S SMALLEST!

Since 2012, the world's smallest chameleon has been the minute *Brookesia micra*, a species known only from an islet off the coast of Madagascar. Adult males grow to just 16 mm long, from nose to bottom, with the total length (tip of head to tip of tail) of both sexes being less than 30 mm.

FLYING DRAGONS

Reptiles evolved around 310 million years ago and soon became the largest predators. They ruled the world for over 200 million years.

During this time, some reptiles took to the air and evolved the ability of powered flight. The pterosaurs (pictured below) were the most capable flying reptiles and several gigantic species evolved and had wingspans greater than 10 m! These were the largest flying animals that ever lived.

A massive meteor impacted Earth 66 million years ago and wiped out all the pterosaurs as well as the dinosaurs and most other groups of large reptiles. No reptiles are alive today that can truly fly, but there are a few that separately evolved the ability to glide!

The forty or so species of flying dragons (of the genus *Draco*) are the most accomplished gliding reptiles alive today!

EXPANDABLE WINGS

Flying dragons are small lizards about 20 cm in size. They live amongst the trees in the rainforests of Asia, and eat insects, ants and termites. They have specialised wing flaps that expand from their sides.

These "wing flaps" (called patagia) consist of six ribs that support a thin skin membrane. Flying dragons can extend their wing flaps outwards or flatten them against their body. Most species also have flaps that extend from their neck or chin which can act as stabilisers.

To glide, flying dragons launch into the air, open their wing flaps and steer or brake with their tails. Many species can glide up to 20 m between trees!

This ability to glide gives flying dragons several major advantages over other lizards. They do not have to climb down each tree and up another in order to search for food, and they can quickly escape from enemies by gliding away.

The males of many flying dragon species are highly territorial and glide to chase rivals away from trees they claim as their own. Many species have bright wing colours and patterns which they flash to rivals as warnings!

FRILLED-NECKED LIZARD

The frilled-necked lizard (*Chlamydosaurus kingii*) lives in northern Australia and southern New Guinea. It can grow up to 1 m long although most of that length is its long tail!

It lives mostly in trees where it searches for insects and other prey, but often comes down onto the ground to forage for food. If the frilled-necked lizard feels threatened, it has a very special trick! It rises on its hind legs, gapes its bright pink or yellow mouth, expands its neck-frill and hisses!

This dramatic show makes the frilled-necked lizard appear much larger than it really is! This startles or scares away many predators. If its warning display doesn't work, the frilled-necked lizard can run really quickly to the nearest tree and climb to safety!

DID YOU KNOW?

- The colour of the frilled-necked lizard's frill varies from yellow to orange to black!

- In the film Jurassic Park, the dinosaur *Dilophosaurus* was portrayed to have a frilled-neck. Zoologists do not actually know if this or any other dinosaurs had frills like the frilled-necked lizard!

SECRET TOADHEAD AGAMA

The secret toadhead agama (*Phrynocephalus mystaceus*) lives in the deserts of Central Asia, mainly in Iran, Afghanistan, Kazakhstan and Uzbekistan. It is far less well known than the frilled-necked lizard of Australia and New Guinea but has a similar trick.

When it feels threatened, the secret toadhead agama opens is mouth, hisses and expands two frilly skin flaps alongside its mouth! The skin flaps are bright pink, red or purple and its broad mouth is also brightly coloured to show off its rows of sharp, white teeth!

If the dramatic warning display isn't enough to scare away an attacker, the secret toadhead agama can bury itself into the desert sand within a few seconds and can remain buried until the danger passes.

Secret toadhead agamas have very unusual tails which they can lift and coil like a scorpion's tail! This may be a form of mimicry to further scare attackers. The end of the tail is tipped in black and used to communicate!

SPECTACULAR SNAKES

More than 3,600 species of snakes are known worldwide. They range in size from tiny species that are 10 cm long (e.g. the Barbados threadsnake, *Tetracheilostoma carlae*) to the reticulated python (*Malayopython reticulatus*) which can exceed 10 m in length and weigh over 158 kg!

Unlike the jaws of many other vertebrates which are locked together, the jaws of many snakes are more mobile and connected with tendons, muscles and ligaments. This allows many snakes to eat meals bigger than the initial gape of their mouths!

TASTING THE AIR

Most snakes have an excellent sense of smell. They may initially smell prey through their nostrils, but then flick their tongues to "taste the air". They have extremely sensitive taste organs in their mouths!

SNAKE VENOM!

Of the 3,600 known snake species, only about 600 species are venomous.

The inland taipan, Dubois' sea snake, Eastern brown snake and yellow bellied sea snake are generally regarded as the world's most venomous snakes. All four of these species can carry enough venom to kill over 100 adult humans and their bites can be fatal within one hour!

Scientists have estimated that up to 20,000 people may die annually from snakes, with most deaths sadly occurring in Sub-Saharan Africa and Southeast Asia.

Fortunately, anti-venom can be created to treat bites of many snake species. Small quantities of venom are required in order to produce the anti-venom, so many snake species are "milked" for their venom!

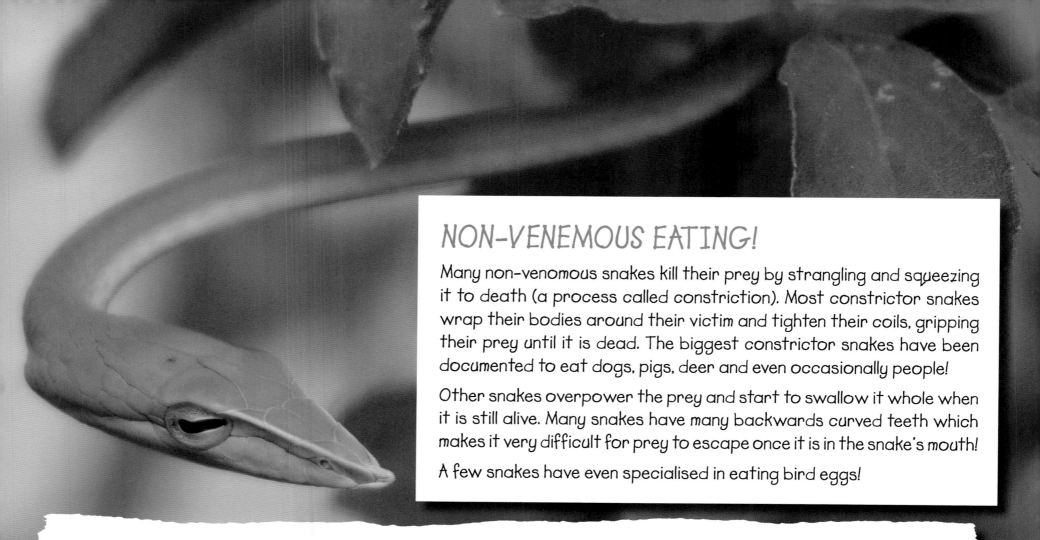

NON-VENEMOUS EATING!

Many non-venomous snakes kill their prey by strangling and squeezing it to death (a process called constriction). Most constrictor snakes wrap their bodies around their victim and tighten their coils, gripping their prey until it is dead. The biggest constrictor snakes have been documented to eat dogs, pigs, deer and even occasionally people!

Other snakes overpower the prey and start to swallow it whole when it is still alive. Many snakes have many backwards curved teeth which makes it very difficult for prey to escape once it is in the snake's mouth!

A few snakes have even specialised in eating bird eggs!

SPOT THE SNAKES

Snakes are masters of disguise! Many species can wait weeks between meals and lie in wait for prey to come within striking range. Can you spot the snakes in the photos below?

DEADLY OR HARMLES

Many of the most venomous snakes have conspicuous colouration to warn enemies to stay away! Other harmless species sometimes have very similar colours and just pretend to be dangerous snakes!

For example, the coral snake (below left) has powerful venom whereas the milk snake (below right) is harmless! The mimicry is close enough that predators leave the milk snake alone! The following rhyme tells them apart: *"red next to yellow, you're a dead fellow; red next to black, safe from attack."*

IRIDESCENT SNAKES

Across the world, many species of snakes have evolved iridescent scales that reflect rainbow-like colours! In most species, the iridescence is caused by iridophores that are present in the scales. The iridophores refract and reflect light, causing the shimmering iridescent effect.

At least thirty species of snakes worldwide have visible iridescence, the most prominent examples being the rainbow boa (*Epicrates cenchria*) from Central and Southern America, the sunbeam snake (*Xenopeltis unicolor*) from Southeast Asia and the white lipped python (*Bothrochilus albertisii*) from New Guinea. Zoologists do not know the reason behind the iridescence, but it may enhance the snakes' camouflage (especially for prey and predators that see in black and white).

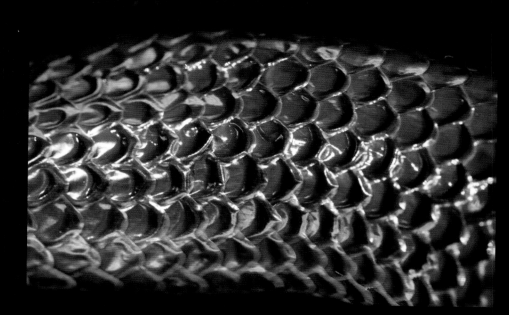

SEA SNAKES

About 70 snake species worldwide have evolved to live in marine environments. These "sea snakes" are fully adapted to aquatic life and have paddle-shaped tails to swim through the water.

Although they may resemble eels, sea snakes do not have gills and must surface regularly to breathe. However, most sea snakes can hold their breathe for more than one hour, with some even being able to stay under water for up to 8 hours!

Sea snakes hunt fish and have extremely powerful venom because they need their prey to die quickly after envenomation, to reduce the chances of it swimming away.

Despite their powerful venom, many sea snakes are not aggressive to humans, and sometimes even seem curious with divers!

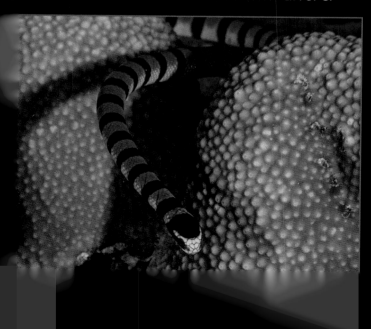

FLYING SNAKES

A handful of snakes have evolved the ability to glide between trees to hunt for prey and to escape enemies. The best known example is the paradise tree snake (*Chrysopelea paradisi*). It launches from a tree, flattens its body and forms an S shape to maximise its aerodynamic lift!

Flying snakes can glide up to 100 m and can partly control the direction they glide in by "slithering" in the air!

SPITTING COBRAS

About twenty species of cobras have the ability to spit venom, which is released from specialised hollow fangs and spurts forward in two jets that can travel up to two metres!

The spitting of venom forms a means of defence, but all spitting cobras can also deliver venom by biting!

All of the known cobras are capable of rearing upwards and expanding the sides of their neck to produce a hood when threatened! This hood makes the snake appear larger and more fierce!

Many cobras can make a very loud hissing-growl as a final warning before it strikes!

DEADLY VENOM!

The venom of spitting cobras is extremely powerful!

Spitting cobras aim their spray of venom at an attacker's eyes. A direct hit in the eyes can quickly cause permanent blindness in humans and even larger animals!

Sadly, many people die each year from unintended encounters with cobras!

PHOTOGRAPHIC CREDITS

The publisher and author would like to thank all those photographers and image makers who have contributed to this book. All photographs are credited to Stewart McPherson except those credited below.

SS = Shutterstock.

Front Cover: Arm001/SS, Nikolai Denisov/SS, toha90/SS, Dirk Ercken/SS, Signature Message/SS, Aphelleon/SS, Tom Smith/SS, Carl Davies/CMD; **i** Joshua Davenport/SS; **ii** Matt Cornish/SS; **iii** JayDM/SS; **1** Positive Snapshot/SS, Antoshin Konstantin/Wikipedia(CC BY-SA 3.0), Silmiart/SS; **2** reptiles4all/SS; **3** Mark_Kostich/SS; **4** Tim Zurowski/SS; **6** Aphelleon/SS, Fotofermer/SS; **7** buteo/SS, Anton Kozyrev/SS, Sanit Fuangnakhon/SS, Dirk Ercken/SS, Chansom Pantip/SS; **8** Daniel Eskridge/SS, Orla/SS; **9** GUDKOV ANDREY/SS; **10** Simia Attentive/SS, udaix/SS, alinabel/SS; **11** Jezper/SS, K_E_N/SS, Ethan Daniels/SS, KYTan/SS, yakonstant/SS, Thomas Retterath/SS, Chansom Pantip/SS; **12** Eric Isselee/SS, serg_dibrova/SS, udaix/SS, Tsekhmister/SS, Denis Tabler/SS, Ekaterina V. Borisova/SS, Eric Isselee/SS, fivespots/SS; **13** Butterfly Hunter/SS, Eric Isselee/SS, udaix/SS, kzww/SS, Marco Uliana/SS, IrinaK/SS, aaltair/SS, Smit/SS, John A. Anderson/SS; **14** Dirk Ercken/SS, VectorMine/SS, desdemona72/SS; **15** Jane Rix/SS, Vadim Nefedoff/SS, Pat Lauzon/SS; **16** RethaAretha/SS, Mark Baldwin/SS, Ondrej Prosicky/SS, Anton Petrus/SS; **17** Sergey Novikov/SS, Simon Dannhauer/SS, neenawat khenyothaa/SS, Arnain/SS; **18** serg_dibrova/SS, Andrea Izzotti/SS, NoPainNoGain/SS; **19** Willyam Bradberry/SS, Lillac/SS, superjoseph/SS; **20** Wanida_Sri/SS, KGrif/SS, Gianfranco Vivi/SS, Valerii_M/SS; **21** Jasper Suijten/SS, DMS Foto/SS, Oliver Osvald/SS, khwanchai/SS; **22** worldswildlifewonders/SS, Dotted Yeti/SS, Alfredo Maiquez/SS, Bildagentur Zoonar GmbH/SS, agus fitriyanto suratno/SS, Tiberiu Sahlean/SS, beachbassman/SS, Arm001/SS; **23** Dirk Ercken/SS, Mr F/SS; **24** Arm001/SS, schlyx/SS, rachata klahan/SS, Lapis2380/SS; **25** Martin Voeller/SS, tristan tan/SS, Nature Picture Library/Alamy Stock Photo/Cyril Ruoso; **26** Michael Benard/SS, Arsgera/SS, Tiberiu Sahlean/SS; **27** both images by Chien C. Lee/WildBorneo.com.my; **28** imageBROKER/Alamy Stock Photo/Fabian von Poser; **29** Viktor Loki/SS, Minden Pictures/Alamy Stock Photo/Minden Pictures, BIOSPHOTO/Alamy Stock Photo/Cyril Ruoso; **30** Dirk Ercken/SS, Valt Ahyppo/SS, dmvphotos/SS, Dirk Ercken/SS, Christian Vinces/SS, reptiles4all/SS, Chansom Pantip/SS; **31** Thorsten Spoerlein/SS, Thorsten Spoerlein/SS, Dirk Ercken/SS, Klaus Ulrich Mueller/SS; **32** Nejron Photo/SS, Fotogenix/SS, PNQ Images/SS, Gowrithas/SS, Neale Cousland/SS, Dicky Asmoro/SS, Ondrej Prosicky/SS, Anton Rodionov/SS; **33** feathercollector/SS, ChameleonsEye/SS; **34** National Geographic Image Collection/Alamy Stock Photo/Tim Laman, Gabbro/Alamy Stock Photo; **35** Minden Pictures/Alamy Stock Photo/Otto Plantema/Buiten-beeld, feathercollector/SS, INTERTOURIST/SS; **36** both images by Ondrej Prosicky/SS; **37** Chansom Pantip/SS, Milan Zygmunt/SS, Ondrej Prosicky/SS, Matt Knoth/SS, Elizaveta Kirina/SS; **38** Vaclav Sebek/SS, Ondrej Prosicky/SS; **39** Evannovostro/SS, JLMcAnally/SS; **40** Ondrej Prosicky/SS, rickyd/SS, HillebrandBreuker/SS, jo Crebbin/SS;

41 Chansom Pantip/SS, feathercollector/SS, teekayu/SS, ehtesham/SS, Dhruba Jyoti Baruah/SS; **42** Lioneska/SS, Kerry Hargrove/SS, Tom Reichner/SS; **43** Jaochainoi1980/SS, Albert Popalis/SS, Wang LiQiang/SS; **44** crbellette/SS, electra/SS, Carolyn Smith1/SS, Zorro Stock Images/SS; **45** Michael Potter11/SS, Johan Swanepoel/SS; **46** Marek Mihulka/SS, Brina L. Bunt/SS, Petr Simon/SS; **47** Jesus Giraldo Gutierrez/SS, Jordi Jornet/SS, Karel Bartik/SS; **48** Jiri Prochazka/SS, Eric Isselee/SS; **49** JeremyRichards/SS, BMJ/SS; **50** nattanan726/SS, Joanne Weston/SS, Krzysztof Odziomek/SS, Tomas Kotouc/SS, bayazed/SS, Redchanka/SS, Serg Zastavkin/SS, Rostislav Stefanek/SS; **51** Dotted Yeti/SS, bluehand/SS, Atypeek Dsgn/SS; **52** both images (c) 2004 Monterey Bay Aquarium Research Institute (MBARI); **53** Paulo Oliveira/Alamy Stock Photo, Kelvin Aitken/VWPics / Alamy Stock Photo, Kurzon /Wikipedia(CC BY-SA 3.0), Dianne Bray/Museum Victoria/Wikipedia(CC BY 3.0 AU); **54** aDam Wildlife/SS, Here Asia/SS, Nicholas Toh/SS, Dwi Agung Sulistyo/SS; **55** Sergey Uryadnikov/SS, Daniel Huebner/SS; **56** Arunee Rodloy/SS, Wlad74/SS, Alina Maieru/SS, slowmotiongli/SS; **57** Sean Pavone/SS, aaltair/SS, archana bhartia/SS, bluehand/SS; **58** Rostislav Stefanek/SS, Paulo Oliveira/Alamy Stock Photo, Gena Melendrez/SS; **59** Paulo Oliveira/Alamy Stock Photo, Ted Small/Alamy Stock Photo, Frank Fennema/SS; **60** Nature Picture Library/Alamy Stock Photo/Doug Perrine, Chaos2Light Images/SS; **61** Martens Tom/SS, Fotokon/SS; **62** Isabel Eve/SS, Rich Carey/SS, Richard Whitcombe/SS; **63** Vladislav Klimin/SS, Azrael3141/SS, Izen Kai/SS; **64** Mirek Kijewski/SS, hjochen/SS, Art65395/SS, CHAINFOTO24/SS, lisnic/SS, Karel Zahradka/SS, lisnic/SS, DiveIvanov/SS; **65** Josephine Julian/SS, Mark Brandon/SS; **66** NoID/SS, Cathy Keifer/SS; **67** tasnenad/SS, sripfoto/SS, nujames10/SS, fivespots/SS; **68** Shaun Jeffers/SS, criskorah/SS; **69** 22August/SS, anko70/SS; **70** Lyu Hu/SS, NoID/SS; **71** JonathanShum/SS, Petar B photography/SS; **72** nicemyphoto/SS, hillmanchaiyaphum/SS, Dennis van de Water/SS; **73** Tanawat Palee/SS, Mark Brandon/SS, VANESSAL/SS, SIMON SHIM/SS; **74** Joe Belanger/SS, YUSRAN ABDUL RAHMAN/SS, blue-sea.cz/SS; **75** blue-sea.cz/SS, Jesus Cobaleda/SS, Francesco_Ricciardi/SS, kathrin_underwater/SS; **76** Mike Workman/SS, Jack Pokoj/SS; **77** Mitar Vidakovic/SS, NoID/SS, Patrick Joseph Krug (both shots of *Elysia chlorotica*); **78** DiveIvanov/SS, Konstantin G/SS, Bas van der Pluijm/SS; **79** Ethan Daniels/SS, koi88/SS; **80** Fotos593/SS, RealityImages/SS, Guillermo Guerao Serra/SS; **81** Dr Morley Read/SS, Uno_Mas_Bajo_El_Sol/SS; **82** Geoffrey Jones/SS, Audrey Snider-Bell/SS, 77Ivan/SS, Arnoud Quanjer/SS; **83** Ryan M. Bolton/SS, Audrey Snider-Bell/SS; **84** RealityImages/SS; **85** khlungcenter/SS, pitaksin/SS, GG6369/SS; **86** Lisa Preston/Indian Ocean Experiences; **87** Minden Pictures/Alamy Stock Photo/Ingo Arndt; **89** KiltedArab/SS; **90** Graham R Prentice/SS, Minden Pictures/Alamy Stock Photo/ : Mark Moffett, Brian Donovan/SS; **91** SIMON SHIM/SS, Pong Wira/SS, Emre Terim/SS; **92** ThomasLENNE/SS, Himanshu Saraf/SS, Claudia Paulussen/SS, Bambara/SS, Beth Ruggiero-York/SS, SkyLynx/SS, Tomas Kotouc/SS, Michal Ninger/SS; **93** Onyx9/SS, Ari Wid/SS, Boule/SS; **94** Thomas Retterath/SS, R J Endall Photographer/SS; **95** Notara WG/SS, Wildnerdpix/SS, tyler 123/SS; **96** Ondrej Prosicky/SS, esdeem/SS, schankz/SS;

THE AUTHOR

Stewart McPherson is a British naturalist, author and film-maker. Fascinated by wildlife from an early age, he began writing his first book at the age of sixteen. Stewart went on to study geography at the University of Durham, and on graduating, he spent ten years climbing 300 mountains across the world (some of which were previously unexplored) to study and photograph carnivorous plants in the wild, to write a series of 30 books. Along the way, he co-discovered and co-named 35 new species/varieties of carnivorous plants, including some of the largest pitcher plants ever discovered.

After featuring in short sequences in several broadcast documentaries, Stewart and a camera team travelled to all of the UK Overseas Territories to document the wildlife, cultures, history and landscapes that the territories harbour. The resulting documentary series was released as *Britain's Treasure Islands* on the BBC, National Geographic, SBS and many other channels. The accompanying *Britain's Treasure Islands* book was distributed widely and (through sponsorship), copies were donated to 5,350 secondary schools and 2,000 libraries.

Stewart works closely with the Don Hanson Charitable Foundation to create and donate educational resources to schools to inspire students' learning and passion for conservation. He helped create and send 10,000 "Hanson Boxes" of resources to UK schools in 2019 and 20,000 in 2020.

www.stewartmcpherson.com

INDEX